R

KT-368-415

Career Planning for Solicitors

BPP Professional Education
32-34 Colmore Circus
Birmingham B4 6BN
Phone: 0121 345 9843

BPP University

104723

Other titles available from Law Society Publishing:

Alternative Business Structures
Miller and Pardoe

Equality and Diversity Toolkit
Mark Lomas

Lexcel Client Care Toolkit (2nd edn)
The Law Society

Lexcel People Management Toolkit
The Law Society

Lexcel Small Practice Toolkit
The Law Society

Regulation and In-house Lawyers
Tracey Calvert and Bronwyn Still

Solicitors and the Accounts Rules
Peter Camp

SRA Handbook
Solicitors Regulation Authority

The Solicitor's Handbook 2013
Hopper and Treverton-Jones

Titles from Law Society Publishing can be ordered from all good bookshops or direct (telephone 0870 850 1422, email **lawsociety@prolog.uk.com** or visit our online shop at **www.lawsociety.org.uk/bookshop**).

Career Planning for Solicitors

Edited by Sue Lenkowski

The Law Society

All rights reserved. No part of this publication may be reproduced in any material form, whether by photocopying, scanning, downloading onto computer or otherwise without the written permission of the Law Society except in accordance with the provisions of the Copyright, Designs and Patents Act 1988. Applications should be addressed in the first instance, in writing, to Law Society Publishing. Any unauthorised or restricted act in relation to this publication may result in civil proceedings and/or criminal prosecution.

Whilst all reasonable care has been taken in the preparation of this publication, neither the publisher nor the authors can accept any responsibility for any loss occasioned to any person acting or refraining from action as a result of relying upon its contents.

The views expressed in this publication should be taken as those of the author only unless it is specifically indicated that the Law Society has given its endorsement.

The authors have asserted the right under the Copyright, Designs and Patents Act 1988 to be identified as authors of this work.

© The Law Society 2013

The Urgent/Important Matrix in Chapter 3 is reproduced with permission from MindTools.com.

ISBN-13: 978-1-907698-69-9
Published in 2013 by the Law Society
113 Chancery Lane, London WC2A 1PL

Typeset by Columns Design XML Ltd, Reading
Printed by TJ International Ltd, Padstow, Cornwall

The paper used for the text pages of this book is FSC certified. FSC (the Forest Stewardship Council) is an international network to promote responsible management of the world's forests.

Contents

Notes on contributors

Julia Bateman is head of international at the Law Society. After completing an undergraduate degree in History and French at University College London (including an exchange year at the Sorbonne, Paris) she undertook a postgraduate diploma in Law and the Bar Vocational Course. After having been called to the Bar in 2000 she went to Brussels for a traineeship in the European Commission, followed by a two-year stint as a political advisor to a UK member of the European Parliament. Julia joined the Brussels office of the Law Society in 2003 and she became Head of EU Affairs in 2008. She moved back to the UK in 2011 after her appointment as head of international.

Dawn Dixon qualified in November 1990 with London law firm William Heath & Co and was made a partner in 1995. She remained with William Heath & Co until cofounding Webster Dixon LLP in 1998 where she remained as joint founding managing partner and head of property and private client departments until 2013.

She is currently engaged as a consultant solicitor with PDC Legal. Dawn was formerly chair of the Association of Women Solicitors (AWS) London Group and the National Group. She is currently a committee member of the Women Lawyers Division.

Dawn has lectured on the AWS Returner Course and the Commonwealth Lawyers Association.

Steven Durno is the policy officer at the Law Society responsible for the administration of justice. That remit includes the Society's policy work on judicial appointments and support for solicitors wishing to apply for judicial office. He also has responsibility for planning and environmental law. He came to the Law Society from local government in 1989.

Ruth Fenton worked as an international business consultant for 10 years before becoming a solicitor in 2007. Ruth has worked for magic circle, US and regional law firms.

Ruth is highly trained in business psychology and corporate strategy and currently works as a legal business strategist with Inspired Star (**www.inspiredstar.net**). Ruth specialises in coaching legal professionals to become more successful and regularly mentors disabled solicitors. In addition, Ruth acts as a mediator and arbitrator through Inspired Resolution.

Ruth has had award-winning articles and papers published in the UK and overseas including in *Law Practice Today* and *The Times* on legal and business topics.

Kat Gibson qualified in October 2005 and has worked in-house since October 2007. She initially worked in an EMEA role for a global telecoms company, but joined Coca-Cola Enterprises in 2009. Kat is an employment specialist and, as such, is proficient in advising on employment law issues, data privacy and compliance matters. While in-house, she also provided advice on marketing, commercial and competition law. She moved back to private practice in March 2013, after almost six years in-house, and is a member of the Employment Practice Group at DLA Piper UK LLP in London.

Melissa Hardee is a consultant with international consultancy, Hardee Consulting, and advises professional service firms, educational institutions and regulators on legal education and training, regulation and strategic development.

Melissa was a training partner at CMS Cameron McKenna before becoming director of the legal practice course at the Inns of Court School of Law. Melissa has chaired the City of London Law Society Training Committee, the Legal Education and Training Group, and the Association of LPC Providers, and currently chairs the Training Committee of the City of Westminster and Holborn Law Society, of which she is also president.

Melissa's new book, the *Legal Education and Training Handbook*, will be published by the Law Society in 2014.

Sue Lenkowski graduated in 1983 with a 2.1 Business Studies degree from Leicester Polytechnic. She is a licensed psychometric tester and member of the Chartered Institute of Personnel and Development (CIPD). The early part of her career was spent in a variety of recruitment, training and assessment roles in local government. In 1997 Sue joined Irwin Mitchell solicitors and spent 11 years as both head of training and development and graduate recruitment. In December 2008 Sue set up her own consultancy business – Sue Lenkowski Ltd.

Sue works primarily in the legal sector on a variety of recruitment and learning and development projects and interim roles. A particular focus of her work in recent years has been the development of alternative graduate schemes and the legal apprenticeship framework. She is also a career consultant at BPP.

Leslie Moran is professor of Law at Birkbeck College, University of London. Birkbeck Law School exemplifies the widening participation mission of the College, providing research-led undergraduate and post-graduate education on a part- and full-time basis. He qualified as a solicitor in 1979. He has worked in a variety of higher education institutions. He has an international reputation for his research in areas relating to the judiciary, visual culture and law, sexuality and law and criminal justice. He has published many articles and books. He is a member of the Law Society's Equality and Diversity Committee and has strong links with InterLaw Diversity Forum for Lesbian, Gay, Bisexual and Transgender (LGBT) Networks, an interorganisational forum for the LGBT networks in law firms.

Kevin Poulter is a senior associate in the employment team of London firm Bircham Dyson Bell LLP. He represents a broad range of companies, charities and NGOs on all employment law issues.

Kevin has a particular interest in social media and frequently advises companies on the implementation, regulation, monitoring and enforcement of social media policies and speaks regularly on this topic.

He is a well known commentator in the legal and business media and has contributed to *The Guardian*, *The Sunday Times*, *LondonLovesBusiness*, *Justice Gap*, *Legal Week* and *The Lawyer* and has appeared on BBC Breakfast, Arise News and local and national radio. He writes a monthly column in the *Solicitors Journal* and hosts a weekly podcast at Legal Cheek.

Follow Kevin on Twitter @kevinpoulter or visit **www.KevinPoulter.com** for further information.

Tony Roe is the principal and founder of niche practice, Tony Roe Divorce & Family Law Solicitors, Berkshire, set up in February 2008. The firm, which regularly appears in the Legal 500 and Chambers directories, offers all forms of family law dispute resolution. Tony is one of the first 60, nationally, to have passed the Family Law Arbitration Course. He is also a trained collaborative family lawyer.

Tony has written on family law and practice management in the *Law Society Gazette*, *Solicitors Journal* and *Butterworths Family Law Journal*, appeared in national and local media and has lectured widely.

Follow Tony Roe Solicitors on Twitter @tonyroedivorce or visit their website at **www.tonyroesolicitors.com** for further information.

Foreword

The Junior Lawyers Division (JLD) encourages lawyers to be well informed and motivated. Being a lawyer today is not only about having the ability to understand and interpret law, to draft, advocate and communicate with clients, it is also about business awareness, marketing and technology. Lawyers further require knowledge of the processes needed to place them in a position that allows them to achieve their career goals and fulfil their expectations. This can be daunting and problematic for lawyers.

We find law in many different places and often we spend hours undertaking research on behalf of clients. Today's lawyers therefore have little time left to research and comprehend the options available to them in the development of their own careers. This book has been compiled to enable the reader to quickly ascertain and understand the many and varied roles open to them.

I was delighted when the JLD was asked in the early drafting stages of this book whether it felt the content was appropriate and useful. The Executive Committee read the early chapter plans and advised accordingly. During the later stages it read the proof and spoke to its members to try to ensure lawyers' needs were reflected in the content.

This enabled the authors to undertake valuable market research and listen to the feedback of the JLD. The JLD's advice was that lawyers need a comprehensive guide that provides factual answers to many questions regarding legal practice and development. The JLD wanted all of the information to be readily available in a single format and to be clear, concise and easily digestible.

This book contains some content contributed by practising lawyers; it is not based purely on academic theory and also refers to real-life case studies and experiences. To that end it is refreshing in its accuracy and practicality.

This book further allows the reader to use its companion website which features an additional chapter written by Peter Wright on career progression. Readers can access this online resource at **http:// juniorlawyers.lawsociety.org.uk/career-planning-for-solicitors**.

I suggest that you read the entire content as each chapter provides answers to questions that you and your colleagues will be asking on a regular basis. Not only are general topics such as marketing yourself, the training contract and career planning included, but detailed advice and information is provided on subjects including setting up a law firm, partnerships and how to work in-house or internationally.

The JLD encourages diversity and understands that many young lawyers struggle to purchase expensive publications. It has therefore subsidised the publication of this book to allow it to be marketed at a reasonable price and thus accessible to lawyers at all stages of their careers.

In a profession which has become increasingly competitive and diverse, lawyers need to be aware of all of the options available to them. They need to be flexible, well informed and knowledgeable. This book is an extremely useful resource that informs, assists and guides you from the beginning of, and throughout, your career in law.

On behalf of the JLD, I wish to express thanks to the authors and contributors of this guide for their hard work, and I hope that you, the reader, find its content valuable in the development of your skills as a lawyer and that it assists you in building a successful and fulfilling career.

Heather Iqbal-Rayner
Chair, Junior Lawyers Division

Chapter 1

Career planning – an overview

Sue Lenkowski

This book covers planning and managing the different stages in a career in the legal sector.

The National Careers Service defines career management as follows (**https://nationalcareersservice.direct.gov.uk/advice/planning**):

> A plan helps you focus on what you should do when thinking about a new career. It also helps if you would like to progress in the career you are in.
>
> Career planning helps realise your ambitions – what you would like to do in your working life. A plan helps you focus on what you should do when thinking about a new career. It also helps if you would like to progress in the career you are in.
>
> Planning needs time and careful consideration. You need to think about:
>
> - what you can do already
> - what you would like to do next
> - what else you need to learn.

In my experience very few people manage and plan their careers in such a systematic way and in the current economic climate the notion that you can achieve both this and financial stability may seem like an impossible dream. However, understanding what you want to achieve and planning how you will get there is something that most people will find invaluable throughout their professional life. But planning alone is not enough; having made a plan, it is important to break it down into meaningful actions. As Peter Drucker said, 'Plans are only good intentions unless they immediately degenerate into hard work' (**www.quotationspage.com/quote/1990. html**).

Career planning is about setting your goal and putting in place actions to achieve it and there are a number of steps involved in this.

Step 1: The structure of your plan

Consider what you want to achieve in your lifetime (or at least, by a significant and distant age in the future).

Once you have set your overall goal, set a five-year plan of smaller goals that you need to complete, then create a one-year plan, a six-month plan and a one-month plan of progressively smaller goals.

You can then create a plan of action of what to do when.

Once you have decided on your first set of goals, keep the process going by reviewing and updating your plan of action; periodically review your longer term plans and modify them to reflect your changing priorities and experience.

Before you can set these there are a number of other steps to consider.

Step 2: Decisions

From an early age we are asked 'What do you want to be when you grow up?' Our answers to this question can change almost like the days of the week and are often based on personal experience or something we have seen on the TV (law is littered with people inspired by programmes such as *Silk* and *This Life* to name just two). The occupations of our parents and siblings also play a major role, as do the people we meet and admire.

For some people, the question 'What do you want to be when you grow up?' never gets fully answered.

For another group of people career ideas formed in youth remain their career plan for life. These people are both lucky and unfortunate in equal measure. They are lucky because they can plan from an early age. This is important as a career plan requires decisions about all aspects of your life, take, for example, A-level choices. For a career in law in the current climate, choosing non-mainstream subjects at A-levels is likely to narrow down opportunities with certain types of firms. These same people are unfortunate, however, because, unlike 40 or 50 years ago, the idea of a job for life is now a dim and distant memory and someone who has only ever considered one career will often struggle to come to terms with the need to switch careers or work in a sector which has changed out of all recognition.

I was one of the lucky/unfortunate ones. I had decided on a career in human resources (HR) from the age of 14 and methodically planned my A-levels and degree towards this aim. I refused to take a straight academic degree at a well-renowned university, choosing instead to take a more practical vocationally-orientated sandwich degree at a polytechnic.

Despite all this planning and focus I had not factored in the economic situation in the mid-1980s and found myself unemployed on graduation. I had to review my plans and for many years found myself in administrative roles in local government. However at least having a plan meant I could constantly make decisions with a clear end goal in sight.

Whether you are in the former category or the latter, it is important to plan or at least evaluate logically and rationally what you are looking to do.

In my experience there are a high proportion of law students (graduates and postgraduates) who have paid limited attention to this step and are surprised and often angry and upset that they can't break into their chosen career.

Chapter 11 of this book, which looks in detail at how to change direction in your career, contains much useful advice that also applies to the initial stages of career planning.

Step 3: Look at yourself

Consider what attracts your attention and what you enjoy reading about, watching or talking about. In other words, what gets you motivated?

Ask yourself, what do you want from your career? Try to go beyond money as this is actually rarely a motivator beyond a basic level. Consider what factors will help you feel motivated to go to work every day. Career values typically identified by students as being important include work that is satisfying, stimulating, and meaningful; work that provides an intellectual challenge; making a difference to people's lives and solving problems. The challenge here is that you need to decide what is satisfying, stimulating and meaningful to you.

I attended a seminar aimed at helping retiring athletes make career choices at the end of their athletics careers. The speaker suggested to the audience that a really useful tip is to think carefully about the things you always do without a to-do list. This is a really simple and effective way for you to answer the question of what motivates you. Try it – you might be surprised at the results.

Think about your personality, for example, do you prefer working with data or people? Do you like to plan and work in a methodical way? Do you prefer ambiguity or structure? Map these traits into the sort of career options available to you. The law has a variety of types of roles which are explored in later chapters of this book and finding a fit for you is critical. Consider what you want and need in a career before looking at specific career paths and specific occupations.

Step 4: Review the routes and roles

Choosing your route used to mean making the choice between becoming a barrister or a solicitor. Both routes required a degree and a postgraduate qualification followed by a period of work-based learning (pupillage and training contract).

In the days when these were effectively the only two recognised roles and the supply of graduates and opportunities for work-based learning were equally matched, at its simplest level, choice was around preference for court work leading to the bar, or client facing activities leading to becoming a solicitor.

The supply and demand equation has dramatically changed however, as there now is an oversupply of students and an undersupply of training contracts and pupillage. At the same time the profession is radically changing with the advent of alternative business structures (ABSs). ABSs are covered in detail in **Chapter 7** but they mean that non-lawyers will be able to own and manage law firms so the drive to be a qualified solicitor may not be as great as in the past.

Running in parallel to these changes, more and more people are considering the Chartered Institute of Legal Executives (CILEx) route into law. The route offers the opportunity to earn and learn simultaneously and a Fellow of CILEx has recognition within the regulatory framework. In addition, Fellows can qualify as solicitors without a training contract.

There are a variety of ways this can be achieved, including without a degree or post-degree, or after you finish school or college. The career opportunities are plentiful and deserve serious thought for those considering entry into the modern profession. The CILEx website (**www.cilex. org.uk**) is a great place to start to explore this route.

A recent development has also been the introduction of legal apprenticeships. These 'new kids on the block' are creating quite a stir. The government-backed programmes currently available to GCSE and A-level students offer an alternative route into the law with the opportunity to obtain National Vocational Qualifications (NVQs) while working in a law firm.

By September 2013, it is planned that NVQs will be available to level 4 (post A-level) with a vision to develop NVQs to level 7 within a further two years. This means that there may be a further route to qualification without a university degree.

So far we have looked at the known future routes, but what about the unknown?

In his most recent book, *Tomorrow's Lawyers: An Introduction to Your Future* (Oxford University Press, 2013), Richard Susskind provides an interesting perspective of the possible new job roles which may be available to those with an initial legal education. He identifies eight new roles, which, if he is correct, will radically change the skill sets and career paths of those working in the legal sector. I would advise all readers to look at these and consider the impact they may have on your career planning.

These developments and changes clearly demonstrate the need to make planning a priority if you are to achieve your career goals.

Step 5: Consider how you match up

The first and most important part of this step is to look at your record of academic achievement.

As the supply and demand equation has changed, this is one of the most critical requirements for the solicitor/barrister route. In the current climate, without strong academic qualifications (minimum 2.1 and A B B A-levels), it is becoming increasingly difficult to obtain a training contract or pupillage. Two or three years ago I met far too many students who had not factored this into their planning and who recognised too late that their career plan was unlikely to be realised. In recent years more and more students are becoming aware of this but I still see far too many who have been naive regarding their chances of securing a training contract.

For the record, it does not automatically mean that without strong academic qualifications you will not obtain a training contract or pupillage as there are some firms that run access schemes and others that will recruit from a paralegal route. But it is a high risk strategy that you need to factor into your planning and it really is critical that you explore all the alternatives before making the traditional route your path of choice.

Step 6: Test out your choice

Do you really understand the pressures and the lifestyle which a legal career involves?

Many students fail to test out their career choice robustly. There is absolutely no substitute for seeing and experiencing firsthand what the job involves. Talk to and meet as many people as possible to gain a 'warts and all' view of what it is like to be a lawyer and what the different types of law and legal practices are actually like.

I often meet students who plan their careers based on where they perceive there are the most jobs or which jobs pay the most money. I meet many students who are drawn to private client work: they love the work and feedback from work experience indicates they will make great lawyers in this area. However many struggle with elective choices, and consider doing commercial subjects believing these will provide them with a passport to a training contract. The most important point about career planning however, is to do something which you will enjoy.

Fifty years is a long time to be unhappy in work so you need to choose to study and practise an area of law you are genuinely interested in and adjust your expectations accordingly. **Chapter 2** gives a great deal more advice on testing out your choice.

Step 7: Set your goals

Having worked your way through these steps now you can start to set your goals.

A useful way of making your career goals more powerful is to use the SMART mnemonic.

SMART stands for:

S   Specific
M   Measurable
A   Achievable
R   Realistic
T   Time-bound

To help you put this into practice, let's look at an example.

Example

It is September 2013 and Jane is about to start the second year of her law degree. Her overall long-term career goal is:

> to be a partner in a top 100 law firm within 10 years of qualifying as a solicitor.

She starts by developing a set of goals for 2013/2014:

- Attend law fair in October 2013.
- By November 2013 review firms she met at the law fair and decide which firms she will make applications to, checking that she is a match for their requirements.
- Apply for six vacation placements before December 2014.
- Obtain and undertake three placements before Easter 2014.
- Make 10 training contract applications by June 2014.
- Obtain a training contract offer from at least one of these firms by September 2014.

Within each of these goals she lists specific tasks she will need to undertake and these will drive her career plan for the year.

You can see from this small extract of Jane's planning diary, career planning requires considerable time and effort but it is the key to success.

You should treat career planning as an additional module of your studies and, for those readers who are later on in their careers, I suggest that career planning becomes part of your professional self-management as well.

Step 8: Continually review and revise your plan

As the legal landscape changes and your personal circumstances change, you will need to constantly re-evaluate your career goals and plans. This book has chapters devoted to helping you to achieve these paths, whether this means taking a career break, moving to a new firm to broaden your experience or seek promotion, working in-house or moving into a non-legal sector role.

So before you rush to start to write your career plan or reflect on a career change, move on to reading the rest of this book.

Chapter 2

What firms look for

Sue Lenkowski

There are numerous publications in which firms detail the specific entry requirements and attributes that they are looking for. It is fair to say that the majority of firms are looking for very similar attributes.

Most common attributes law firms look for

Good academic qualifications

Increasingly firms will be looking for a robust and consistent record of academic achievement. In reality this means looking back to GCSE and A-level grades as well as degree and postgraduate performance. It is not impossible to secure a training contract with a 2.2 or poor A-levels but the odds are stacked heavily against you. Yes, some firms will accept mitigating circumstances or have an access scheme, but embarking on a legal career with anything less than strong academic grades requires considerable reflection.

Commerciality/commercial awareness

No matter what area of law or type of firm, commercial awareness is of paramount importance.

I used to run an assessment centre which featured a written exercise that required candidates to undertake a basic profit and loss calculation before making recommendations on future growth strategy. After 10 minutes into this assessment a candidate left the room. The candidate told me 'I can't do this, I just want to be a criminal lawyer'. I responded at the time, and would assert even more firmly now, that an understanding of finance and business matters is critical to practising all areas of law including criminal law in a climate of legal aid reductions. I hope this candidate reflected on the experience and worked hard to develop this skill.

Personal skills

There is a consistent list of skills which firms are looking for. A typical list will include:

- team work;
- resilience;
- logical thinking and analysis;
- interpersonal skills;
- negotiation skills;
- attention to detail;
- organisation and time management;
- ability to work under pressure; and
- common sense.

The most important lesson a candidate can learn is that it is not enough to simply list that you have these skills but rather you need to provide recruiters with clear evidence of where you have demonstrated them. The rationale behind competency-based questions on application forms and in interviews is to test this out. In the absence of specific questions, you should always include in your covering letter the skills which you have and provide the evidence.

Desire to work for a firm

Despite understanding that very few candidates will only apply for one firm (I would suggest this is would be a very risky approach), firms want you to demonstrate that you really want to work for them.

Many candidates think repeating the brochure and/or information on the website will do this. Having spent late July weekends for many years ploughing through 1600-plus applications, I can honestly say it will not! I wrote the brochure that you are quoting from and therefore at best your answer will be boring and at worst unimpressive.

Candidates need to demonstrate that they have thoroughly researched a firm and then relate what they know to their own experiences and motivation for making an application.

Fit with culture and values

A much more subjective and potentially controversial criterion is 'Fit with the culture and values of a firm'.

The apparent cliché marketing message of many firms is that 'We are different' and having worked with a variety of firms this is absolutely true in terms of culture. There have been many occasions in my career where I have found myself working in a firm and wondering if I was still working in the same sector.

But how do you find out if you have a cultural fit? A work placement is a fantastic opportunity to assess the reality of a firm's culture beyond the marketing hype. In addition, prior to making applications, I often suggest to students that they attend law fairs and view trainee profiles on firm websites and ask themselves the question, 'Do I feel similar or different to the people I have read about or met?' If the answer is 'Different', then maybe, just maybe, you are not a fit with that firm.

This statement may seem counterintuitive to the current drive for diversity within the profession, of which I am a huge supporter, however it is a useful place to start. I would also recommend looking at the ways that each firm is embracing the diversity agenda.

Knowledge and understanding of the legal sector

Firms will expect candidates to have both an understanding of the key issues facing the legal sector in general and the issues facing their particular client base.

At a recent presentation to a sixth form college I asked the students, 'What is an ABS?' Most looked blank but one young man answered this perfectly. In contrast, an LPC graduate, who when asked at interview, 'What do you understand by the term "Tesco Law"?' responded, 'It's a new set of regulations regarding shelf stacking'. I know which of these two candidates is more likely to succeed!

Of course that is an extreme example, however, firms do want to see that you have knowledge of what is happening in the sector. You also need to understand how the sector will change over the next five years as this may impact your decision to choose a career in law. Some commentators suggest that the traditional law firm model may be an antique within the next five years so not keeping abreast of the changes is a very dangerous thing to do and may lead to a very unhappy career.

It is also not enough to just have knowledge of the changes – you will need to be able to articulate and substantiate your views on the changes to the sector and client base and what their impact may be.

Knowledge and understanding of the commercial sector

If you are making applications to become a commercial lawyer, firms will want to see evidence that you have a genuine interest in, and an understanding of, the commercial world.

A classic application or interview question is, 'Tell us about a recent commercial news story'. Candidates who struggle with this type of question may want to ask themselves whether they have what it takes to enter this area of law and/or should certainly start to take an interest in commercial matters.

Work experience

Trainee solicitor recruitment is quite a bizarre and unique process. Recruiting two years in advance makes recruitment decisions very risky and so firms are increasingly using their work experience programmes to 'test' for the skills they are looking for. Observing a person in the working environment for a week or two is a far better predictor of job success than an assessment centre or interview.

That aside, firms are also looking to see that students have work experience elsewhere as evidence that students have tested out their career choice and also as a way of providing examples of the key skills they are looking for in candidates.

All work experience – legal or non-legal, paid or voluntary – can be valuable. Bar work, for example, can provide evidence of client handling skills, commerciality, working under pressure and team work. Voluntary work can be an indicator of similar skills but can also be used to demonstrate commitment and a fit with a firm's values.

The key is demonstrating these skills in an application, which is covered in greater depth in the next section.

So, armed with the information about what firms are looking for, let's move on to how you market yourself.

How to market yourself

When I present at student forums or provide careers advice, I always begin a discussion about marketing by looking at a normal distribution curve (see **Figure 2.1**).

In all my years in graduate recruitment the predictions always hold true. There will be a small percentage of candidates (10–20 per cent) who can almost instantly be rejected: they fail to meet the minimum academic criteria, fail to complete the form correctly or have poor spelling and grammar. There will be a small percentage who stand out (10–20 per cent) and the vast majority will be typical/average/okay.

Graduate recruiters are faced with the perennial problem of how to select graduates from the 80 per cent who all look the same. As the demand side of the market shrinks and the supply side increases, this 80 per cent becomes larger every year. Students who present themselves as typically decent/average candidates are unlikely to succeed. Typical is no longer enough.

Moving yourself from typical to good (into the top 20 per cent of the curve) is the key and great marketing is the answer.

So, how do you market yourself? In this section I want to introduce you to the business concept of the 'marketing mix' (see **Figure 2.2**).

I was introduced to this concept during the early days of my business studies degree. At the time I used it as a tool to analyse the best approach to market a service or product but the concept can equally be applied to

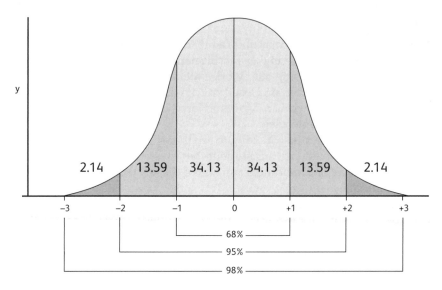

Figure 2.1 Distribution curve

marketing yourself to law firms. Treating yourself as the product you wish to sell and analysing how to do this, just as in the business world with a new product, is a great approach.

So let's take each P in turn.

Price

It is unlikely that you will be able to dictate this, however, I am often faced with students who base their marketing strategy on salary, choosing only to apply to firms who pay upper quartile rates at trainee and newly qualified (NQ) level. If this is a key driver for you, look carefully at what these firms require and ensure you really match what they are looking for, then follow the rest of the mix. If not, maybe you need to reassess.

Place

The key questions to answer here are:

- Where are you looking to sell yourself geographically?
- What type of firm do you want to work for?
- What area of law do you wish to practise?

Often students will have answers to these questions but, when challenged, have either little or no substantial reasons for their choices. The key to marketing yourself is to be able to demonstrate to a firm that you have thought through your reasons, tested out your choice and that your skills and abilities are a great match with what the firm is looking for.

In terms of geography, it has become increasingly important to demonstrate clear ties and commitments to the geographical location. I know of one firm that shortlists using evidence that candidates have local contacts and an understanding of the local market. Put bluntly, if you have lived all your life in Manchester and you are making an application to Southampton, you need to convince a firm why you want to live and work there.

Figure 2.2　The marketing mix

Product

The product is you. Ultimately you need to have a series of strong and robust reasons and evidence why a recruiter should 'buy' you rather than another candidate.

Many students find this a difficult exercise. A starting point might be to think about why you bought your latest smartphone over all those on the market – what were the key features that swayed you? Once you have done this you may find it easier to analyse yourself in a similar way.

Start by considering the following key questions.

What are my strengths? What are my weaknesses?

Your answers to these questions need to be backed up with a range of examples preferably from different life experiences to date. In relation to weaknesses, beware of clichés such as 'I am a bit of a perfectionist'.

What are my unique selling points (USPs)? Why am I different from other students?

I have seen examples of students using their USPs in applications but in the end becoming memorable for the wrong reasons. The one I remember most clearly is the student who went into great detail about her love of pole dancing on an application form. Yes, this was different but the image I had in my head was not one which placed her in the top 20 per cent. Try to think of what USPs you may have that will add value to the firm.

Do I have or can I develop the attributes which the firm is looking for?

This final question is critical. There is little point making applications to firms that are looking for qualities or experience which you do not have. You really need to challenge yourself and ask yourself, if you were the recruiter, would you consider that your experience and examples are strong evidence that you have the attributes that they are looking for?

Sometimes this is really easy. I once met a student who had to detail her prizes and awards for academic achievement in 250 words. The student said she was struggling as she didn't have any. My suggestion was that as she didn't have these, and the firm had a substantial section devoted to detailing them, that maybe she would not be a suitable candidate and she should concentrate on other firms.

Promotion

This is the big one, and the most important part of your marketing strategy.

How can you promote yourself to a law firm?

Some good ideas are to:

- attend law fairs, look smart and ask a few pertinent questions;
- attend presentations/events on campus and ensure you network with presenters after the event;
- get a place on a mentoring scheme with your target firm(s);

- join the Junior Lawyers Division (JLD) and network with trainees and newly qualified solicitors from your target firms; and
- use your university careers service to refine your applications.

But don't:

- stalk recruiters and staff by sending multiple emails;
- try to make your application stand out by adding quirky additions (e.g. using coloured paper); and
- exaggerate your skills and experience.

At the Manchester Law Fair in 2012 I told a few students the following tip which they said was the best tip they had ever heard, so assuming they weren't just being polite here it is:

Law is a very small world and it never ceases to amaze me how many people know a person in other firms, either through their professional or personal lives. So always speak highly of every firm and person you have met, always create a positive impression with everyone you meet in whatever context and always assume that the person you are talking to knows other people who know you.

Cultivating and maintaining a network

So in this very small world of law how should you go about cultivating and maintaining a network?

If you are genuinely interested in developing a network, the first thing to realise is that it will take time and you will need to give it priority alongside your studies and leisure activities. The first step is to identify existing networks and then prioritise those which will be most beneficial to you.

The two main networking opportunities which I would recommend all students get involved with are the JLD and campus events and presentations.

Junior Lawyers Division (JLD)

The JLD was set up as a specific group within the Law Society to provide junior lawyers with support, advice, information and networking opportunities.

It operates on both a local and national level and offers a great way of networking with students and practioner members (both trainees and qualified staff). It can provide careers advice, social and networking events and the opportunity to influence the future of the profession.

I have known a number of students who have taken on committee roles at both national and local levels in the JLD and have subsequently secured training contracts by being able to demonstrate key skills developed as a result of their involvement. Others have found it a great way to get 'inside' information on what firms are looking for and sometimes informal mentoring or placements with firms. Attending JLD social events is a fantastic and enjoyable way to meet people from a wide variety of firms and will help you broaden your knowledge of the issues facing the profession and gain valuable insights and tips.

Campus events and presentations

Many firms run events and presentations at universities and postgraduate law schools. These are 'priority number one' networking events for you to attend. Not only will you be given lots of useful information about how to apply to a firm and what a firm is looking for, you will also have the opportunity to make an impression with recruiters which you may be able to use as part of your USP when making an application. I cannot stress strongly enough the value of these events and presentations.

When you attend firm events always wear business attire and ensure you have practised three key messages to get across to the people you meet at the event to make sure you are a memorable potential candidate. Make a note of the names of the people you speak to directly and follow up your attendance at an event with an email thanking them for their time. It can be tempting to spend time speaking to people you already know at networking events, for example, just talking to careers tutors or other students but remember your aim and make sure you speak to people you haven't met before. Don't be afraid to introduce yourself – I find a smile, handshake and brief introduction such as, 'Hi, I'm Sue, I don't think we've met yet', can often be an easy way to strike up a conversation.

One point about handshakes: too many students have either a weak or limp handshake or look, frankly, terrified when I proffer my hand. A firm confident handshake is a must as it is your first impression and I suggest you practise this before attending any events.

Other networks

There are so many other potential networks that it is hard to detail them all in this book, but consider local societies, for example, the Medico Legal Society if you are interested in clinical negligence, relevant local pressure groups and alumni events/newsletters at your undergraduate university. Also remember to keep in touch with old tutors and peers.

If you want to network with members of your local business community, Junior Chamber International (JCI) operates in most cities and can be a great forum to develop both your skills and knowledge.

Finally, whatever networks you choose to engage in, make sure you use a contact management tool to record emails, phone numbers and everything else you can about the people you meet. There are many apps on the market to help you do this quickly and easily on a smartphone or tablet.

Networking using social media

Social media is a fantastic way to network and has revolutionised the way that people stay connected.

Before looking in detail at LinkedIn and Twitter, here is some general advice about the use of social media.

Consider your social media presence very carefully. Unless you really lock down your privacy settings on Facebook, you can find your professional reputation at risk with people in your professional network having access to photos and information which you wouldn't want to be shared. Try doing a simple Google search on yourself and you may be both amazed and horrified at the information that is out there! If that's the case you need to start by cleaning up your online presence and locking down your security. This is great general advice as more and more employers are looking at candidates' online presence and you may find that a fun night out costs you the opportunity of getting a job.

LinkedIn

One of the best business networking tools is LinkedIn which is an online directory of professionals and companies.

Individuals and companies use LinkedIn for networking, job searching, hiring, company research and connecting with co-workers, including alumni, industry and a variety of other business-related groups.

The starting point for using the network is to create a profile.

Your profile should be as detailed as possible and should include the following:

- A photo. If people see your profile without a photo they are less likely to connect with you as they may not be sure that it is you. The photo should be one in a professional context, not from your holidays or nights out, and make sure it is recent.
- Your education history.
- Work experience, both paid and voluntary.
- Keywords and skills. Include all the keywords and skills from your CV in your profile. This will make it easier for your profile to be found in search results.
- A headline, because it will appear at the top of the page when someone views your profile and can dramatically increase your contacts.
- Your career aspirations.
- A professional summary as this is a great way to highlight your experience and what you are looking for.

After you have set up your profiles, you should do the following:

- Create a LinkedIn signature to use in your email. That's another way to increase the visibility of your profile.

- Update your profile. Your profile should always be current and up to date.
- Grow your network. Connect with other members and build your network. The more connections you have, the more opportunities will become available, but don't randomly connect with people you don't know. All that does is annoy them and you won't gain anything from it.
- Get recommendations. To a potential employer, a LinkedIn recommendation is like a reference.
- Regularly post status updates, not the 'having my tea' variety but post commentary on important events and links to interesting articles about the sector. Remember to always make sure that what you're posting presents a professional image and one that will stand out to employers in the legal sector for the right reasons.
- Join relevant discussion groups. These will not only provide you with useful up-to-date knowledge of important issues in the sector, they will also allow you to connect with others in the sector.
- Follow firms. Many firms have an account that you can follow. If you do this you can always be up to date with the latest news in the firm.

Twitter

Many students hold a Twitter account to follow footballers, celebrities and their friends but if you limit your Twitter activity to this then you are missing a fantastic networking opportunity.

All the mainstream legal press have Twitter accounts and following these makes keeping up to date with the sector really easy and I would encourage any student to do this.

In addition, many firms have Twitter accounts that are often written by trainees so following these is a great way to get under the skin of a firm. Some firms also announce deadlines and vacancies via their Twitter accounts and some offer competitions to win placements. So make sure you follow your preferred firms.

If you do decide to use Twitter, be aware that anyone can see your tweets. So if you want to use Twitter for social interaction then make sure you protect your tweets or, better still, create a separate account for your non-work persona.

Chapter 3

Getting the most out of your training contract

Sue Lenkowski

If you are reading this chapter before starting your training contract, my first piece of advice is to remember how you felt when you received the letter, phone call or email making you the offer. At that time a sense of relief was probably your number one emotion – you had secured the elusive training contract and you were on your way to achieving your career aspiration of becoming a solicitor.

Why do I mention this? Because in my experience some trainees forget this feeling and they arrive on induction with an attitude that they have already made it. They sometimes forget that the critical word is 'training' and they are at a firm not to learn just legal skills but organisational/life skills as well, which will form the foundation of a successful career.

I once worked with a training principal who used to begin her slot on the induction course with the following statement:

> You were smart enough to convince us at the interview that you had the qualities we were looking for, now comes the hard part – showing us that you have those qualities in practice.

Sensible trainees will be wise to remember these words.

So how do you get the most out of your training contract? **Figure 3.1** highlights the key points.

Seat rotations

Seat rotations (short-term spells spent in different areas of practice) are the most common way that learning is structured in a training contract. Whether the seat rotation is four seats, six seats or more informal, you are required to have covered criteria laid down by the Solicitors Regulation Authority (SRA).

Seat moves are the aspect of a training contract which trainees, HR/graduate recruitment, supervisors and partners probably dislike the most.

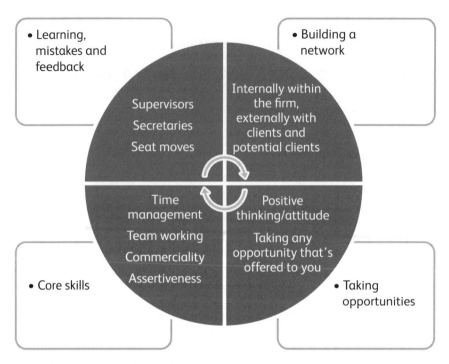

- Learning, mistakes and feedback

- Building a network

Supervisors
Secretaries
Seat moves

Internally within the firm, externally with clients and potential clients

Time management
Team working
Commerciality
Assertiveness

Positive thinking/attitude

Taking any opportunity that's offered to you

- Core skills

- Taking opportunities

Figure 3.1 What you can gain from your training contract

From an HR/graduate recruitment perspective, seat rotations are a thankless task. It is virtually impossible to take the wishes of trainees and the SRA requirements, with respect to areas of law and contentious/non-contentious split, map these onto the needs of the business and make everyone happy.

Tip 1: Be flexible

If you want to get the most out of your training contract, accept that you may need to be flexible in your choice of seats and if you do not get a seat of your choice, remember studying law and practising law are poles apart and always move into a seat with an open mind.

I remember placing a trainee in a Court of Protection seat. This trainee did not want to go there as he wanted to be a criminal solicitor but he needed to get non-contentious experience to complete his training contract. He made his views known to me in no uncertain terms. After three months in the seat the trainee contacted me to explain that he no longer wanted to qualify into criminal law as he wanted to be a Court of Protection lawyer.

This anecdote illustrates that until you try an area of law you cannot decide if it is for you. Of course, quite often you will complete a seat and have your gut reaction confirmed that it is not for you but if you go into a seat with a negative view then it will almost certainly show in your attitude and quality of work. Your next supervisor may be told about this and it will not help you to create a positive first impression.

Tip 2: Do not harass HR/graduate recruitment

Trainees who bombard HR with emails and calls about seat moves tend to be remembered for the wrong reasons. You will be told when the plans are finalised, in fact, I personally never want anything more than to release this information, so don't hassle HR.

Waiting to find out is great preparation for what will follow in the rest of your legal career, for example, when you will be waiting to find out if you have a job on qualification, made associate or made partner. These often all involve long and protracted decision-making.

Tip 3: Keep a learning log

The SRA requires you to keep a learning log for very good reason: it's a fantastic way to map your development and, just as importantly, it can help you to identify your transferable skills and decide on the direction you want to take on qualification (see **Chapter 4**).

Supervisors

One of the major challenges of a training contract is that if you are training at a firm that operates a traditional seat rotation you will work with at least four to six direct supervisors and teams during your two-year training contract. This can often feel daunting and some trainees say a training contract can feel like having a new job every six months.

Tip 1: Try not to be too hard on yourself

Recognise that your confidence may dip when you move into each new seat. It's normal and natural and so long as the confidence dips become smaller as you go through your training then you're on the right track.

Tip 2: Adapt your way of working to fit with your supervisor's style

In my experience, trainees sometimes find it hard to adapt to working with different supervisors.

One guaranteed way to have a difficult time in a new seat is to fail to adapt your way of working to meet your new supervisor's style.

Before you start with a new supervisor or at the beginning of your first seat consider doing the following:

- Email the supervisor and say how much you are looking forward to working with his or her team. Even if you did not get the seat of your choice it is never a good idea to say this. Go into the seat with an open mind and determined to get as much out of it as possible.
- Ask if the supervisor would like to meet you before you start the seat and consider sending your up-to-date CV if your HR team has not done this for you.
- Ask if there are any specific areas of law that you should get up to speed with before you start the seat.
- Ask if there are any particular clients you should research before starting.
- Give him or her any pre-arranged course dates/holidays.

As soon as you begin a new seat ask your supervisor the following:

- How would he or she prefer you to ask questions – by email or in person?
- Are there particular times of day when he or she does not wish to be disturbed?
- If you are struggling with something in the team, should you go to HR directly or would the supervisor prefer you to ask him or her?
- How does he or she like to be updated on matters – by email or in person?
- What are the qualities he or she looks for in his or her trainees and what is he or she looking for you to be able to show?
- Is there a particular set of team rules about office cover during lunch breaks?
- Are there any fixed dates for team meetings or team training, etc.?

Finding out this information from your supervisor should really help you get off on the right foot and create a good first impression but there are also many other people who can provide you with information about your new team, notably the legal secretaries.

Secretaries

Many legal secretaries have been with their firms for a long time and are fantastic sources of information, support and guidance. This will not be the case however, if you treat them as second class citizens or deal with them in a manner that suggests you are superior.

Many qualified solicitors talk about buying flowers when a secretary helped them, taking them out to lunch, remembering birthdays and holidays and asking about the family. Of course these are great tips for working with all your team members but, as legal secretaries can be your lifeline, making sure you treat them well is vital.

I once worked at a firm where one seat had the so-called 'X test'. X was the name of the secretary and her job was to spend half an hour telling the trainee about the team members and how they worked. If the trainee passed the 'test' by looking interested and speaking to her as an equal she would help him or her during the six months and also inform the team that the new trainee would be okay. If a trainee failed the 'test', the secretary would pass this information on to the rest of the team and also make sure the trainee's typing went to the bottom of the pile and would delay answering questions and providing support.

Mistakes

At the beginning of this chapter I highlighted the point that a training contract is about training and learning. As such you will spend a large proportion of your training contract making mistakes and dealing with criticism/feedback.

In terms of mistakes there are some very simple tips below.

Tip 1: Own up

Honesty and integrity go to the heart of what it means to be a solicitor so never try to conceal a mistake as it will always be found out.

You may find it hard to believe but even the most experienced solicitors occasionally make mistakes and their advice will always be tell someone, take the flack and then work together to rectify it. You are more likely to be reprimanded for trying to cover up the mistake than for the mistake itself.

Tip 2: Choose a good time

Try to find a time when you know your supervisor will have sufficient time to listen to you and agree a course of action. Trying to discuss a mistake when your supervisor is packing his or her bags to go home will probably be unlikely to lead to a productive conversation.

Tip 3: Be direct

Get straight to the point: tell them what you have done, what you think the consequences are and, where possible, what you think the solution might be. The old adage 'don't come to me with problems; come to me with solutions' always holds true: busy people don't have time to listen to your story about a sleepless night or how much you drank last night in an effort to stop worrying.

Tip 4: Be professional

Different supervisors will react in different ways. I have worked with some who remain unnervingly calm, others who rant and rave and all behaviours in between. Whatever your supervisor's reaction is, stay calm, don't cry and don't try to make an excuse as the time for the post mortem is after the mistake has been rectified.

Tip 5: Don't repeat the mistake

Most supervisors will forgive a mistake but what really makes people angry is if you make the same mistake again. Correcting mistakes costs time and time is money so learn from your mistakes and show you have done so.

Feedback

Your training contract will be a process of continuous feedback.

Trainees who learn to react positively to feedback are the ones who learn most from the experience and stand out at the end of the training contract.

I can recall trainees who at the end of their training contracts still refused to acknowledge the feedback they had been given. It was always someone else's fault, a personality clash or the area of law, etc. These trainees failed to get the most out of their training contracts and as a result would certainly not have been the best lawyers.

So the following tips may prove useful.

Tip 1: Value constructive criticism

Adopt the mindset that you will never learn if you don't seek feedback and take it on board.

Tip 2: Listen

Often feedback will hurt but seek to clarify what is being said to you by asking questions so you can genuinely understand what you need to do differently.

Tip 3: Avoid becoming defensive

It is a natural reaction to become defensive and either dismiss criticism or retaliate but the more you do this, the less you will learn.

Tip 4: Agree action

Seek constructive changes that you can make to the issues which prompted the criticism and agree alternative action and/or behaviours in the future.

Networking

A training contract is a great internal networking opportunity. Trainees generally know more people across a firm than partners do.

As a trainee make sure you keep in touch with as many colleagues as possible and don't restrict your networking to your trainee peer group. Attend 'knowhow' events and engage in pro bono social and charity activities as well as laid on networking events. This will help you understand the whole business, not just the teams you have worked in, and can be a vital and highly valued knowledge base that you can use to potentially provide cross selling opportunities to your colleagues. This is really important, particularly in larger firms, and something which will not go unnoticed by your supervisors.

'Work hard, play hard' is a phrase which many firms use in their graduate recruitment literature and, while it is a bit of a cliché, it does have an important message. Be careful, however, as social activity should not be at the expense of getting your work done and showing dedication and commitment to your team. Yes, if you have been the key to a firm's social circle, people are likely to notice and remember you but at the end of your training contract you will be judged on your ability as a lawyer.

External networking is a skill which trainees should look to develop over the course of their training contract as it is at the heart of any successful law firm.

In the first meeting I had with a partner in a criminal part of the firm, the partner asked if I would like to see his tools. He proceeded to open his desk drawer which was filled with boxes of cigarettes. This, he said, is how he wins over clients. This example is a bit extreme and clearly not something that would be acceptable today but it illustrates the point that networking plays a part no matter what type of law you practise.

Trainees may be asked to get involved in networking in a number of ways. Some of the most common include:

- joining local groups, for example, JCI or young professional groups;
- attending conferences;
- acting as hosts at drinks evenings;
- attending training sessions at the firm's offices;
- writing briefing notes for a firm newsletter;
- attending local colleges and schools;
- volunteering for charity events; or
- writing and delivering presentations.

So what are the most important things you can do?

Preparation

Do your preparation before any networking event – find out who will be attending and make it your business to know as much about them as possible. The internet has made this a much easier task than in the past. Review their LinkedIn profiles, read articles they have written and, if they are business people, make it your priority to find out as much as possible about their business and the issues facing the sector they are in.

Armed with this information, decide who you are going to speak to and make sure that you ask them some well thought out questions based on your research.

Prepare three key messages about yourself and the firm that you will look to get across in the conversations that you have. Preparing your opening statement will reduce your nerves and help you come across as confident and relaxed.

If you have business cards make sure you take these and have them readily at hand.

At the event

The most common mistake at events is to talk to people that you know. This is never an appropriate way to behave at an event.

It is true that most people love to talk about themselves so circulate round the room and ask people what they do, how they got into that business, what they know about the firm and use it as an opportunity to help people see how the firm could help them.

Another common mistake is to talk to only one person. Don't be afraid to move on to talk to other people at the event but make sure you introduce the previous person to someone else and explain you need to say hello to x or y.

Some firms will advise that you pair up with another colleague to network and work the room together. Asking your firm if you can do this is a great idea, particularly if you can be paired with a more experienced and senior colleague.

There is often alcohol present at networking events and, without wishing to sound patronising, never use the opportunity of a free bar to get intoxicated even if some of the clients do.

After the event

Be sure to make a note of everyone you met and key points about your conversation (as previously mentioned, smartphones are fantastic tools to use for this) and, where appropriate, drop your contacts an email saying how much you enjoyed meeting them and any follow up actions you agreed to take.

I cannot stress enough how important it is to develop your networking skills during your training contract. As your career progresses, it is likely to require you to concentrate more on client relationships and networking so the earlier you start the better. Networking is a highly valued skill and it will certainly be noticed by your supervisors.

Time management

Time is money and never was this phrase more accurate than in a law firm.

Learning how to manage your time effectively will make your training contract a lot easier to manage and the skills you learn will be invaluable for the rest of your legal career.

Many students are asked a competency-based question at the interview about managing their time and conflicting priorities. Answering this during an interview and the reality of the situation are often far apart.

So how do you manage time effectively?

Unfortunately, there is no magic wand to slow down the ticking of the clock but there are some tips and techniques that can help you manage your time.

Before we look at those, however, I want to talk about personality types. There are some people who prefer to work in a highly planned and organised way: they love to-do lists and they plan in time to work on projects/matters well in advance. They are the sort of people who hate last minute changes. Then there are others who enjoy the adrenalin buzz of completing tasks at the last minute and find detailed planning a chore. These two personality types often clash in the workplace and this is even more extreme when they are in a manager and subordinate relationship. Both personality types find the other frustrating, however both can be equally as productive and there is a place for both in the workplace.

The following tips are adapted from Mind Tools (**www.mindtools.com/pages/article/newHTE_91.htm**). When looking at the tips below remember they are not applicable to every personality type so decide which may work for you. What is important is that you find a way to work on multiple matters, hit deadlines and apply a cost benefit to everything you do, ensuring that you recognise that for the fee involved you need to adjust the time spent accordingly while ensuring a quality output.

Tip 1: Urgent versus important

The urgent/important matrix is a powerful way of thinking about priorities. Using it helps you overcome the natural tendency to focus on urgent

27

activities, so that you can keep enough time to focus on what's really important. This is the way you move from 'fire fighting' into a position where you can grow your career.

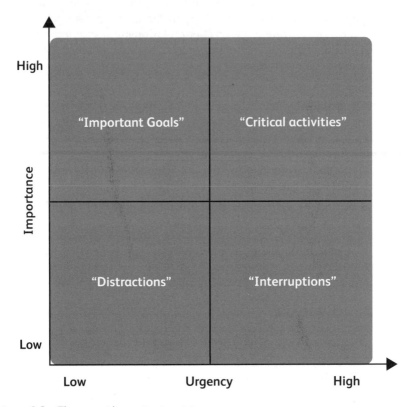

Figure 3.2   The urgent/important matrix

Follow the steps below to use the matrix to prioritise your activities:

1. List all the activities and projects that you feel you have to do. Try to include everything that takes up your time at work, however unimportant.
2. Next, on a scale of 1 to 5, assign importance to each of the activities.
3. Once you've assigned an importance value to each activity, evaluate its urgency. As you do this, plot each item on the matrix according to the values that you've given it.

Strategies for different quadrants of the matrix

- **Urgent and important**

  There are two distinct types of urgent and important activities: ones that you could not plan for and others that you have left to the last minute.

  You can avoid last-minute activities by planning ahead and avoiding procrastination.

  Issues and crises, on the other hand, cannot always be foreseen or avoided. Here, the best approach is to leave some time in your schedule to handle unexpected issues and unplanned important activities. (If a major crisis arises, then you'll need to reschedule other events.)

  If you have a lot of urgent and important activities, identify which of these could have been foreseen, and think about how you could schedule similar activities ahead of time, so that they don't become urgent.

- **Urgent and not important**

  Ask yourself whether these tasks can be rescheduled, or whether you can delegate them.

  Common sources of 'urgent and not important' tasks are other people in your office. Sometimes it's appropriate to say 'no' to people politely.

- **Not urgent, but important**

  These are the activities that help you achieve your personal and professional goals, and complete important work. Make sure that you have plenty of time to do these things properly, so that they do not become urgent.

- **Not urgent and not important**

  These activities are just a distraction, and should be avoided if possible. Some can simply be ignored or cancelled. Others may be activities that other people may want you to do, but which do not contribute to your own desired outcomes. Again, say 'no' politely, if you can.

Tip 2: Email

Email is a wonderful tool and has revolutionised the way we work. It is, however, a thief of time. How many times a day do we stop what we are doing to check an email that has come in? For many of us it can be 50-plus times a day. Assuming that each email interrupts our thoughts by one minute and it takes us one minute to refocus on what we are doing, that is a loss of over 1.5 hours a day!

Adopt the following way of working in your professional career now. Set aside three blocks of time during the day for checking emails and turn off the message notification, then see how much more productive you can be.

Some people throw up their hands in horror at this – what if the email is urgent? Rest assured, if it's urgent someone will phone you.

Tip 3: Learning to say 'no' – be assertive!

Many trainees think they cannot say no so they start to take on more and more work and inevitably they start to work longer and longer hours and/or miss deadlines and produce sloppy work. None of this will be impressive to their supervisors.

So learn to say no in a positive way. If someone gives you an additional piece of work, share with them your workload and your concern. They may decide to reprioritise your work, give you a different way of undertaking the work or look for someone else to help.

Never take on a piece of work that you can't complete within the deadline and if you think you may struggle to meet one, the earlier you can let your supervisor know the better. This is the professional thing to do and not a sign of weakness.

Tip 4: Commerciality

Always be aware that the amount of time you should spend on a piece of work is driven by the fee involved. A common mistake of trainees fresh out of law school is to spend far too much time on matters. If in doubt ask your supervisor and colleagues and make it your business to understand the charging structure of the work you are doing.

Tip 5: Staying late

Law is not a 'nine to five' job and all trainees will find themselves occasionally working long hours, often through the night, in transactional work. This is simply the nature of the work, however, some trainees think it is important to stay in the office long after the demands of their work require. They have the idea that this will be valued.

In my experience this is not the case, particularly as you will find it difficult to record your time on a job so that it can be justified in a commercial way. In addition this type of behaviour may often trigger a question in your supervisor's mind that you are not coping, so don't be afraid to leave the office if you have completed your tasks for the day.

Teamwork

Tip: You don't have to like everyone you work with

This is a vital skill and one which again you will have faced questions on during the recruitment process. The most important tip here is to learn that you will work with people that you don't like who may also not like you. You may not choose to socialise with these people but you must learn to work with them. Most importantly, try to avoid gossiping about them and moaning to others as this has a nasty habit of getting back to people and will not be conducive to your happiness and success at work.

Take opportunities and be positive

Everyone will have a different experience on their training contract. The type of firm, the people and the economic climate will all impact the opportunities a firm presents to you. I want to stress that it is vital to take all the opportunities that are presented even if at the time you can't see the benefit.

Quite often you will be asked to attend activities outside core working hours, both ones that are quasi-social and ones that are more business-focused. Always try to take up these opportunities even if it means putting your social arrangements on hold.

A conference with counsel starting at 5.30pm may clash with a vital football match for your team, but if you turn it down it gives the impression that you lack the drive and commitment and I know many supervisors who, faced with this situation, will never ask again.

Of course there will be times when you have arrangements that are important and I am not advocating always cancelling your social life but think carefully about the opportunity you are being given and the impression a refusal may give.

Finally if you find you are having a less than positive experience on your training contract, use your support network. Talk to other trainees, friends and family and use your HR contact and the JLD. This is a period of training and it may not all be plain sailing but talking to others and sharing your issues will help you deal with difficulties and ensure you get the most out of your training contract.

Chapter 4

The young lawyer

Sue Lenkowski and Kevin Poulter

Part A: Qualification: what do I want to do? – *Sue Lenkowski*

Your career as a qualified solicitor starts a long time before you submit your forms to the SRA and receive your practising certificate.

The completion of a training contract is not the end but the beginning of a further series of career choices and decisions. The messages of **Chapter 1** are as important after your training contract as they were when you were making your applications.

The majority of trainees start to grapple with the challenges of qualification early in the second year of their training contract. As soon as their qualification date is less than 365 days away, the question of what to do on qualification begins to occupy a large proportion of trainees' waking (and often non-waking) hours.

Some trainees find the decision relatively easy as they have undertaken a seat in an area which they have really enjoyed. The only question for these trainees is: 'Will I be offered an NQ role in this area by my firm or will I need to start looking elsewhere?' Other trainees have either not particularly enjoyed anything or, conversely, they have enjoyed everything. In these circumstances, how do you make the decision of what to do on qualification?

Unfortunately there is no set of rules to help with this dilemma. I recall a trainee who, after his four seats, was of the opinion that he would enjoy a career in any of the areas of law that he had experienced (including unusually both contentious and non-contentious work). His approach to this dilemma was to take the stance that he would see who made him an offer and let fate take its course. What happened? The inevitable happened. He was offered the opportunity to qualify into three different teams. After we had a number of discussions about it, he went with an emotionally-driven choice to work in the team where he felt most comfortable. It was a fairly niche area and his decision could have backfired but I was exceptionally pleased to hear he made partner in this area with the firm with which he trained.

In a situation where a trainee has not really found an area of law which feels like a fit, a similar decision may be appropriate, i.e. taking a reactive approach to the decision and see what is offered.

An alternative is to use networks and contacts to explore other areas of law. I have always encouraged trainees in this situation to ask supervisors and colleagues where they see their strengths to help with the decision-making process.

There is, however, one point which I wish to make about this decision which is, although it is often seen as a final decision, this is not always the case. It is possible to 'choose' an area of law on qualification and subsequently switch over in the first few years after qualifying (as seen in the case studies of **Part C** of this chapter).

I remember a trainee who was keen to qualify into insolvency but on qualification there were no opportunities in the firm where he trained. He was, however, offered an opportunity in a personal injury (PI) team. His initial reaction was to reject the opportunity and look for NQ roles outside the firm. After I explained the culture shock of qualification and how this is amplified by moving to a new firm, he decided to accept the PI role and build his NQ skill set (the vast majority of which is generic) while keeping both in touch with the insolvency team and abreast of legal developments in this area. After 18 months he moved into the insolvency team and is now building a successful career as an insolvency lawyer. This anecdote serves as evidence that you do not necessarily have to make a once and for ever decision on qualification.

In smaller firms the question of specialisation may not really have such significance. Training contracts at smaller firms are often characterised by a less structured and formal experience without 'seats' and often a trainee's decision will be whether to leave on qualification or stay and build a career based on the primary work sources of the firm.

Should I stay or should I go?

Decisions you need to make include:

- Do I stay with firm I have trained with?
- Do I look to join a similar sized firm?
- Do I move to a different size of practice?
- Do I look to move from the public sector to private practice?
- Do I move from private practice to an in-house role?

Again these are not easy decisions but the general advice is that if you can stay with the firm where you trained, this will help you deal with the massive changes that qualification brings. Never underestimate how hard it is to deal with a change of working environment. Later in this chapter we discuss what the new skills and pressures which come with qualification add to this. The first few months as a qualified solicitor will be incredibly stressful anyway so for this reason many trainees will choose to stay at a firm and move on after one year plus post-qualification experience (PQE). Firms often prefer this too as it is easier to develop an NQ who has trained at the firm rather than a lateral hire who will inevitably take time to get up to speed with the working practices of the firm.

If you cannot stay with the firm then my advice is to recognise the pressure that moving practices will create and do not allow your confidence to be dented in the first few months.

Can I move to a different type of firm?

As training contracts are hard to find, many NQs train in firms which are not an ideal fit to their career goals, so can you move to a different type of firm?

Subject to the caveats above, it is perfectly possible to do this. An NQ from a high street practice may sell his or her diverse and highly flexible experience to a large firm by demonstrating that he or she has a unique skill set not seen in the firm's 'home grown' trainees. NQs from large firms may sell their highly specialised training working with leading lawyers in their field to a smaller high street practice as a great 'add value' proposition. Many medium-sized regional firms look to recruit NQs from large city firms recognising they will have received first class training but are looking to redress work/life balance. Trainees who have impressed on a secondment in-house may realise they have more to give as a lawyer business advisor in-house rather than a lawyer to a multitude of clients.

As these examples demonstrate, the most important thing to do is 'sell' your qualities to prospective employers and always bear in mind the NQ culture shock.

The NQ culture shock

Qualification is an amazing moment. All the study, applications, open days, pro bono activity, vacation placements and long days and sometimes nights suddenly seem worthwhile. You have your practising certificate on the wall (or desk in these days of open plan), you sign letters and correspondence as a solicitor and you have distributed your business cards proudly to family and friends. You are now a solicitor.

Unfortunately for many NQs this euphoria is relatively short lived.

Qualification brings some huge challenges. The first is often the realisation that the safety net of being a trainee is no longer there. The buck, to some extent, stops with you. You now have huge professional responsibilities and many NQs feel paralysed with fear. Can I sign this? What are the implications? Is my advice to junior colleagues correct? Do I know the answer? Can I ask others? Suddenly it feels like the safety net provided by supervising solicitors, HR and the trainee peer group has disappeared overnight.

All NQs need to recognise that this may happen and ensure they build support mechanisms to cope with the inevitable moments of self doubt. The need to network and keep in touch with your trainee peer group is critical. It is not a weakness to admit to these challenges and in doing so you will gain valuable support in finding your way through the first few months of your qualified career.

Another culture shock can be having your own targets. Some trainees may have spent their training contracts watching and supporting others achieve targets, but the challenge of having your own is often very stressful (both fee earning and in business development). There is no magic formula for handling these but many of the tips in **Chapter 2** on workplace skills will help you find your way.

Finally, don't underestimate the challenge of dealing with the different ways that people in the firm see you and behave towards you. This challenge is similar to that faced by a newly qualified supervisor in any profession who was previously just one of the team. Suddenly the team go out for team lunches/nights out together without inviting him or her, they choose not to share information and they question unpopular decisions, pointing out that he or she 'has changed'. It's a lonely and uncomfortable place to be. An NQ can face similar challenges and learning to move on from the position of trainee can be hard. Again recognising this is likely to happen and building a support network is vital.

The issues discussed so far in this chapter are fairly generic and cover the typical questions/issues which NQs face. Kevin Poulter offers the view of the practitioner below.

Part B: The young lawyer: a practitioner's perspective
– Kevin Poulter

As you near the end of your training contract, you begin preparing yourself for life as an NQ. Like taking the stabilisers off your first bike, you will be left with only a reassuring hand on your back, encouraging you from behind but allowing you to decide the direction. It may feel like you are being left to your own devices to make your own decisions and mistakes (and you will make mistakes), but you are still likely to find that reassuring hand guiding you when you need it.

You may have spent the last five years or more working towards qualification and now you are here it may feel like an anticlimax. You don't get a medal or any more letters after your name. You have really only just reached the beginning. That said, before you contemplate your future, take a moment to sit back and congratulate yourself. If you have succeeded in securing a solicitor role on qualification you have probably reached your professional ambition – or at least one of them. Celebrate your achievement with a new suit, a holiday, a new pair of shoes or a fancy pen! But don't get carried away as ahead of you are some challenging times. You may feel overwhelmed, out of your depth, alone, underappreciated and even question your choice of career. All these things should pass.

Responsibility and accountability

The biggest change on the move from trainee to NQ is almost always the increased responsibility. You will now be responsible for your own clients and for your own advice. You also take on a greater accountability to your partners, your department, the firm and the SRA. You are no longer able to defer responsibility to your supervisor or whoever has conduct of a particular client or matter. You are no longer able to rely upon the checks and balances made by your supervisor and you will be left to make your own mistakes.

Perhaps for the first time, you will build your own professional reputation. Over the next few months and years you will begin to make a name for yourself within your firm, with clients and also within the wider profession.

Building and maintaining relationships with key colleagues in your firm is important, if not essential, to your own career progression. Equally, however, if not arguably more important, are the relationships you make with clients and potential referrers of work. As your career develops in private practice, you will learn that maintaining such relationships will in due course bring its own reward. A strong network of contacts which are more than just 'connections' on LinkedIn or business cards lying abandoned at the bottom of desk drawers can provide introductions to new clients, new opportunities and help build a strong foundation for the future. Although you might not see the benefits in the first few years, a professional relationship will become mutually beneficial over time.

Key to your success will be how your clients perceive you. This is about more than just the advice you provide. It will take account of how you look, how you carry yourself, your confidence in meetings and how you communicate in person, on the telephone and by email. You may at times feel the need to 'act' as though you are a solicitor. You may think, albeit subconsciously, what would my client expect from a solicitor in this situation? This might not leave you for some years, but over time (and through practice) you will soon feel comfortable in your new solicitor skin.

Of course, client perception is something which changes over time too. As you progress through your career from solicitor to associate and maybe on to partner, clients will expect something more from you. Much of what is expected will come from the experience you gather. Sometimes, it might even be the client's perception or expectation which needs to be corrected. It will be up to you to determine the balance of what is required of you and of them.

You will also be responsible for proper file management. This should be consistent with the firm's policies and the regulatory framework governing your firm and the general conduct of matters.

Being your own person

Almost overnight, you will go from acting on behalf of your supervisor, under his or her control and direction, to acting autonomously and with primary responsibility for your actions. Being a solicitor does not mean acting in isolation though. You will still be part of a team and should not hold back from asking questions, adding to debate or seeking out the advice of your colleagues and superiors. Your colleagues will not expect you to be the complete package immediately. They will remember, some better than others, their own experiences of qualification and learning to work independently. You shouldn't give the impression of being reliant upon them, but it is better to ask questions before acting than trying to rectify mistakes later.

It might be common sense, but you should not think of yourself or your work in a vacuum. Shared ideas and knowledge around the office will lead to more effective, commercial advice than a number of individuals working in silos. Clients will receive better, more considered advice this way and you will have learnt more from the experience.

Your relationships with support staff and with the continuing and new trainees will also change. One minute you are working alongside the first year trainees and the next you will be delegating work and giving them direction. This change in dynamic is often difficult to manage. For most of us, it is natural to want to be liked and to get along with our colleagues. This is not mutually exclusive from having respect for other people and their positions. You may have to suffer a period of unpopularity to gain respect in your new role, however, never forget to treat others the way you would like to be treated yourself.

Time recording and billing

You will already be familiar with time recording as a trainee, but it is likely your hourly rate will have increased upon qualification and you may consider that the price is too high for the level of service you are providing. This is the wrong mindset and setting fee rates, in any case, is not your decision. Your firm and partners will have put considerable thought into setting an appropriate charge out rate and you should aim to record your time accurately. If you have any concerns about how much time you are spending on a particular project or query, these can be addressed with the client partner at the time of billing. You should not be making any decisions to discount your time or billing. This is usually a partner's responsibility and any queries they have can be raised with you before a bill is presented.

For the first time, you will have a billing target against which your performance will be measured. You may even have a bonus dependent on your success against any target. Although targets might not be new to you as an NQ, you should always aim to satisfy your firm's expectations of you. Career progression, amongst other things, will be dependent upon these targets, however arbitrary.

Early specialisation

The legal profession is constantly developing and shifting focus. Usually this is down to demand, but can also be the result of changes to legislation, regulation or increasingly deregulation of the sector. In recent years, the recession has unsettled many firms. Lawyers have been recruited en masse and have specialised in a particular area to meet high demand. For example, the growth of commercial property in a dominant commercial property market during economic boom years led not only to the closure of several high profile firms but also to the loss of hundreds if not thousands of specialist commercial property solicitor jobs.

While you are an NQ, you should try to gain as broad and extensive an experience as possible in the area of practice into which you have qualified. Resist, so far as is possible within your firm, narrowing your field of specialisation too early. Despite the move in recent years towards boutique firms practising in a niche area, junior lawyers must first learn the general lessons of their area of work. A broad client base and client management experience is also essential to future success.

Another concern may be the type of firm you work at, either during your training contract or on qualification. Historically, many partners in the provinces have started their careers in the city, worked for a few years and then moved out of town to join firms at a senior level. They may have taken a client or two with them, but they have made a lifestyle choice to move away from a deep-rooted billing and long hours culture to something that suits family life more.

There remains the opportunity to move between different types of firm, for example, from high street to medium-sized commercial, but rarely to leapfrog a rung in the 'traditional' private firm hierarchy. The movement towards alternative business structures (ABSs) could open up opportunities for movement but, at the time of writing, this is far from certain. As has been the typical concern with a move in-house, there is a risk that a move to an ABS may mean that you are restricting yourself for future moves by becoming too comfortable too soon or even 'typecasting' yourself as a certain type of lawyer. Alternatively, the ancillary skills you may develop at an ABS may set you apart from the typical candidates seeking to further their career progression.

Fundamentally, you are now in the legal profession and ahead of many who started out on this path but have failed. Whatever your choices, it is unlikely that the profession will limit your ambitions moving forward. Indeed, there may be many new opportunities afforded to you, waiting to be seized upon and made your own.

Part C: Changing direction

As is pointed out above, your initial choice of specialisation may not limit your ambition or ultimate path. The final part of this chapter details some case studies of those who have changed direction.

CASE STUDY: High street to in-house

Tell us a little about yourself (where you practise, what type of firm, what work you currently undertake)

I am over eight years' qualified and currently work in-house for a housing association (HA), therein dealing with various property queries but also looking at funding work for this particular HA. I am looking to build an in-house legal team, as like all companies at the minute, we are looking to cost-cut, and therefore bring external legal costs right down with the benefit of an in-house legal team.

What specialism/practice area did you initially gain?

I did some initial experience and subsequently my training contract at a high street firm in northwest London, thrown straight in at the deep end and expected to float. The areas of work I did during this time were immigration, civil litigation, conveyancing, family and criminal.

What specialism/practice area did you develop?

I qualified at this high street firm, however I was subsequently made redundant and thought that I really wanted to carry on with family law, as I really enjoyed it. However, the positions that were coming available were conveyancing/property positions, so therefore this became my 'specialism'.

How did you achieve this?

I took a position at a high street firm at London Bridge doing property work, and subsequently obtained a position at a Legal 500 firm in central London acting on behalf of housing associations and lenders. I continued to be thrown in at the deep end at both of these private practice firms and expected to float!

How long did it take?

I qualified in 2005 and just used the knowledge that I had to grow and grow and I have been working in property for over eight years.

What did you find positive about the experience?

Looking back, as strange as this may sound, I learnt the most from being thrown in at the deep end and to be honest it has made me a more rounded lawyer. I now work with an amazing set of people, who aren't solicitors or barristers, however I am able to use all of the knowledge and skills that I have learnt over the years in my current position.

What was not so positive?

I didn't have the support of a good manager at my two London firms. I was often too conscientious and therefore worked 24/7, while they did exactly the same, when quite clearly there was enough work to fit a team of six solicitors (there were only two of us). However, I do think that because of this experience, I am a much better manager for this.

Also, being torn to shreds by a tribunal judge for turning up on my first day at court (my first day in my training contract) unprepared! However, once again, quite a character building experience!

What is the one thing that you wished you had known before changing or, indeed, before specialising?

Nothing really for me. However, if I was due to qualify now, I would seriously consider all of the options out there, such as working in-house. A lot of companies these days are starting to look to recruit in-house legal teams to drive down external legal costs.

What was the most difficult thing about changing your specialism/practice area?

To keep going when times were rough. I actually considered a career change and to go into teaching.

What tips would you give anyone else thinking of changing their specialism/practice area?

Consider all of your options, don't just jump because things are tough. If you can, do a secondment.

Feel free to ad lib or give any other comments you may have

There is light at the end of the tunnel. I would love to have had the benefit of all of this information when I was going through some really rough patches. It is not easy to break into the legal world with all the competition out there. Keep going though, someone will give you a break. If you know the area that you want to specialise in, go and get some experience (even voluntary) – at least you have shown that company that you are a hard worker and can deliver when asked. They may even consider a permanent role for you, or at least recommend you to someone who is recruiting.

CASE STUDY: Regional firm to local authority

Tell us a little about yourself (where you practise, what type of firm, what work you currently undertake)

Prior to law school I undertook extensive periods of work experience (two to three months at a time) with a medium-sized regional firm. The firm had a corporate drive and a focus on marketing alongside fee earning work. I secured a training contract with the firm and remained with them two years' PQE. I left the firm to move to the South East as by then my husband (not a lawyer) was based there and his area of work gives him limited options to work elsewhere in the country.

Around that time the Legal Services Commission (LSC) contracts were being appealed and private practice family law opportunities were limited. Still post Baby P, local authorities were crying out for care specialists. I initially worked as a locum for a county council and then secured a permanent position with one of the smaller London boroughs. I stayed there for around a year and a half and I moved to one of the joint legal services (advising more than one borough).

What specialism/practice area did you initially gain?

I qualified into family law, divorce (some high value), separation of cohabitants, contact/residence, domestic abuse and care proceedings.

What specialism/practice area did you develop?

While in private practice I was caught between two partners: one specialised in high value divorce and the other in complex contact/residence, care proceedings and domestic abuse. This gave me a great opportunity to develop both areas. I was encouraged in both areas to undertake as much of my own advocacy as possible.

I developed good links with local domestic abuse organisations and became a trustee for a young mum's charity. I headed up my firm's 'Young Marketing Group' for our region.

When I switched to local authority work I continued to undertake public law child work, but now for the applicant. I advised on s.7 and s.37 reports for private law child work (something I particularly enjoyed having been on the receiving end of such reports), Judicial Review (JR) and policy. I also undertake some adult work in support of colleagues. I continue to do my own advocacy as far as possible.

How did you achieve this?

I initially took a position as a locum to gain local authority experience. I already had a good grounding in public law child work (from the respondent's view) but had to develop a better understanding of local authority procedure and regulations and focus more (and try to get the client department to focus) on preparing cases as the applicant. I hadn't previously done JR or policy advice but have always liked trawling through case law to refine points of law/prepare arguments so was happy to pick this up.

How long did it take?

I got my first locum position quite quickly through an agency, but I did have a strong background in this area of law to rely on. I worked as a locum for three months for a county council before moving to one of the smaller London boroughs on a permanent contract. As mentioned above, I stayed there for around a year and a half and then, as I wanted to be part of a larger team and on the look out for development opportunities, I moved to one of the joint legal services.

What did you find positive about the experience?

My knowledge on local authority practice and procedure, and having to deal with advice on finer points of case law will serve me well whether in private practice or local authority work in the future.

I like being the applicant. I like driving cases forward and (hopefully) being in a good position to prepare my case. When I was in private practice dealing with this area of work I did feel frustrated that, acting for respondents, I was often in a reactive position and felt I had less impact on decision-making for children.

Long-term benefits such as flexi working and more holiday are great.

What was not so positive?

The attitude between private practice and local authority. Each regards the other with some degree of suspicion. Being caught in the middle of the two (neither private practice nor local authority) and knowing when I turn up to court I will be viewed as the bad guy. Although, from the start I have actively tried to show those representing respondents that I have an understanding of their pressures (particularly from the LSC) and want to work with them in a positive manner, obviously without prejudicing my client department case, and I am now finding positive responses to this approach.

What is the one thing that you wished you had known before changing or, indeed, before specialising?

Just like private practice firms there are significant differences between different local authority legal departments in size, structure, support, resources and culture. Unlike private practice firms, there are less publications and guides (such as the training contracts guides, etc.) to give you info or insight into the different departments. I felt like I was going into the unknown. Luckily my locum role was with a well-recognised county council and I am now working for one of the combined borough legal departments. Checking things such as whether a department has Lexcel or other practice standards is a good start.

What was the most difficult thing about changing your specialism/practice area?

The transition was more about understanding the change in culture, the complexities of advising and representing a 'we' instead of an 'I' (i.e. local authorities consist of many people trying to work together but on occasion pulling in different directions). It was also about refining my knowledge on local authority procedure and social work practice (understanding my new clients, what they are doing, what they aren't doing and what they're supposed to be doing and how to balance this with what they want to do), and not getting drawn into internal politics or clashes of personality within the client department.

What tips would you give anyone else thinking of changing their specialism/practice area?

If possible, talk to those who have already done it (a good start is reading this book). Think about and focus on what you do know rather than what you don't, but at the same time don't try to blag a specialism – it's really obvious to those already in that area of practice that's what you're doing.

Remember that if you are employed by a local authority legal department your role is to advise the local authority, but you are not the local authority, you are still a solicitor and advise and then act on instructions accordingly.

Additional material available

Please see the JLD website for more material, including an additional chapter covering career development for solicitors by Peter Wright, available at **http://juniorlawyers.lawsociety.org.uk/career-planning-for-solicitors**.

Chapter 5

Partnership

Dawn Dixon

For many aspiring lawyers, the success of one's career may be measured on:

(a) whether you become a partner in your own practice;
(b) whether you are offered partnership in an existing practice; and/or
(c) at what age you become or are offered partnership.

For some, it is seen as a natural route to progression, for others it is an albatross around their necks and to be avoided. Partnership status can be the making of your career but if the decision is taken too lightly and is not well thought through, it can be the breaking of your career as the professional and personal ramifications are endless if it goes wrong.

The second half of this chapter looks at the legal position and regulations which are critical once you have made the decision but initially we need to consider whether becoming a partner is right for you.

Forming or joining a partnership: key considerations

The following questions apply to partnerships pursuant to s.1(1) of the Partnership Act 1890 (hereinafter referred to as s.1(1) partnerships), partnerships under the Limited Partnership Act 1907, limited liability companies (LLPs), limited companies and ABSs.

As s.1(1) of the Partnership Act 1890 confirms, a partnership is a 'relationship'. Like a marriage, a business partnership is a personal relationship which is inevitably based on trust but has public and private ramifications if things go wrong. Unlike a marriage however, you can set out the parameters for consideration in a document reflecting that relationship, before you embark upon it. You may not wish to sit down with your intended spouse and trawl through a list of questions to govern your future life together (unless you enter into a prenuptial agreement) for fear of taking the romance out of the relationship. Forget the romance in a business partnership. It is just a business relationship and do not ever go into it with someone you are not prepared to sack or move on from. I hope a similar state of mind is not adopted in your personal relationships!

I joined William Heath & Co as a trainee in 1988, I qualified in 1990 and became a partner in 1996. I joined a s.1(1) partnership while at William

Heath & Co. I left William Heath & Co to open my own practice, Webster Dixon, in January 1998. Although it was originally a s.1(1) partnership, it became an LLP in March 2003.

My tips represent my practical advice drawn from my experience with both types of partnerships and my general experience of professional business life. I hope they help you to avoid the pitfalls on your pathway to progression through your career and please remember the following:

- You must enter the business relationship with your eyes wide open not shut.
- You must adopt an open dialogue (at the beginning and continuously throughout).
- You must prepare and reduce your discussions to precise and clear documentation so you are able to ease your way out of the partnership if necessary. You are lawyers and why should the cobbler's children wear the worst shoes? You would not advise a client to enter into a business relationship without an agreement. So why do it yourself?
- You may not be a commercial lawyer, nor know someone who is, but I am sure you can buy a book or otherwise employ a lawyer to help!
- When you consider my advice please always remember the five Ps: 'Proper Preparation Prevents Poor Performance'.

Consideration 1: The term

You should only consider a partnership if it is a mid to long-term plan for you. Do not join or create one as a stepping stone to something else as the ramifications on leaving, or the partnership going sour, could affect you for years to come and it is not to be taken lightly. If you have to join a partnership for a short period, make sure you have completed your due diligence so that you can effortlessly remove yourself from the business if necessary, with limited liability being attached to you.

If you are considering a s.1(1) partnership, ensure you have sufficient indemnities in writing from the existing partners to ring fence and protect yourself and your assets.

At this juncture we should consider the position of salaried partners. There has been a steady growth of salaried partners so that the equity partners can share the management load of the business without giving up any real power. Very typically, you will have someone who is very ambitious, intelligent, young and professional, who has served his or her traineeship and believes he or she is entitled to the status and prestige of being a partner, without having the capital or the necessary experience to become an equity partner. This person will be represented as a partner to the wider public and to clients and his or her name will appear on the notepaper and of course, his or her business card will confirm the same. This individual will bind the firm in the same way as a full partner, however, within the partnership agreement which governs the relationship to the other partners, the person's ability to earn may be restricted to a fixed sum and paid as a salary. This salary would be paid out of net profits meaning that he or she takes the risk of the outgoings of any year preventing him or her from being paid.

Consider the salaried partner route as it may be a way of testing your wares before you buy them!

Consideration 2: Values/ethos

Do you and your partner(s) share the same values/ethos? This is important regardless of whether you are joining a small, medium or large practice. What are the values of the business and what are yours? Do they match? Will you be moving in the same direction or pulling away from each other? What is the firm's business plan? If you are joining a national practice, how do you know what all partners are thinking and how they should behave? Are there checks and balances and rules and regulations which apply to the partners to prevent too much divergence? In a two-partner LLP, it is easier to work out the values and ethos of your partner but it is not bulletproof and questions still need to be asked.

Consider the following:

- What type of hours do the partners keep?
- What amount of billing do the partners achieve?
- How much work, administration and marketing are you all expected to carry out?
- What is, or will be, the firm's culture?
- Can you be a library lawyer, just doing work and no marketing?
- Must you go out and bring in the work in order to sustain your practice and the partnership?
- Can you achieve this?
- What are the other skills that you can contribute to the partnership if you cannot bring in work or contribute money?
- Do you have partners to work 'in' the business (administration) and those to work 'on' the business to allow the business to grow (marketing, PR)? All firms require administrators and visionaries.

Consideration 3: The six needs

Every person has a dominant need. When I employed an agent/consultant within my practice, she highlighted some points and suggested that I carry out the following test in my private and public life, in order to get a true understanding of my needs as well as those of my business partners, my staff and those people around me.

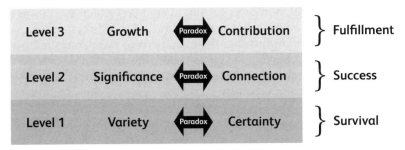

Insatiable Paradox

Figure 5.1 The six needs

(A) Certainty

Everybody requires certainty in his or her life. This includes security/survival and the ability to avoid pain and discomfort and gain pleasure. With reference to your business, employees obtain certainty as they know (or should know) if they do a month's work, they will be paid, this is for certain. If you have good rules and regulations in your business you should not suffer claims if there are checks and balances. We require this certainty in life to have someone there to depend on. However, also consider the opposite.

(B) Uncertainty

We also need a certain amount of uncertainty in our lives and this includes surprises, challenges and variety. This is one of the most important of the needs but it must be in the correct quantity. Too much uncertainty can be destructive. In your personal life, if your partner is erratic, this uncertainty could destabilise your relationship. If he or she constantly surprises you in a good way, this is good uncertainty. In a professional relationship, if you have any business obstacles, the uncertainty may be good for business as it may stir the imagination and add adrenalin which could be a good thing for the partnership.

(C) Significance

This refers to importance, recognition, uniqueness and the 'need to be needed'. However, you must have the right type of significance and not be significant for the wrong reasons. In which camp do your partners fall?

(D) Love and connection

We require love from our home and family and connection from our work. This refers to the sharing of relationships that we encounter every single day. We need to be connected to our businesses either as the owners wanting it to grow and protect it or as employees feeling a connection to the place that employs them and pays them. You do not want your staff to have no connection to the business at all as they will carry out their tasks in a mundane fashion without any thought for the future of your business and this will affect the business culture.

(E) Contribution

This refers to the giving and receiving, the involvement and inclusion, and action and motion. Contribution is important in both your private and professional relationships. How can you get your partners and staff to contribute to the business and do they want to contribute? What can they contribute? Everybody needs to be given the opportunity to contribute and if they do not then they may feel no connection as in (D) above. What strategies can you devise to ensure that all partners contribute as well as staff? How often have you felt that a staff member has made a contribution but has not put that comment forward until they were asked and the contribution almost extracted from them because someone in your group had too much of (C)!

(F) Growth

This refers to achievement, movement in a forward direction and progression. You need to grow in your private life and professional career through promotion and progression within your business.

Understanding your partner's dominant need

There is paradox between needs (A) and (B) and therefore the mix and quantity must be right. In terms of needs (C) and (D), success depends on how significance is gained, it must be gained in a positive way, to build 'love and connection'.

If you assess (A) to (F) correctly and identify the dominant need within your business and private relationships, you will hopefully assess that each person has a dominant need. If you can work out which is your partner's dominant need then you can work towards respecting that need as it relates to yours and vice versa. All contributions may hopefully allow your business to grow.

Consideration 4: Conflict resolution

This is one of the most important considerations to ask of your prospective partners but probably one of the most difficult to get the truth. I would suggest that you devise a questionnaire to be answered by all the partners before you agree the terms of any agreement. It is almost akin to psychometrically analysing your partners before you buy in. The questions should include but are not limited to the following:

- How does your prospective partner(s) deal with conflict in his or her professional and personal life?
- Does his or her style sit well with your style of dealing with and resolving conflict?
- In times of stress, how will your intended partner(s) behave? Will he or she stay on course, cut loose and run or throw the toys out of the pram?
- How will his or her reactions, good or bad, affect you and how will you behave?

If things go wrong, these question tease out how you may expect your partner to behave with you. Ask these questions in order to provide clues on how your prospective partner may behave if things go bad. These clues may give you the true picture of his or her mental and emotional state. It is only in adversity that you will see the true measure of a man or woman. You do not want to be surprised!

Consideration 5: Give 'you' a chance

It is important to give the partnership life and, therefore, you must make the partnership work, perhaps by making it less favourable to leave or quit. The key is not to make it impossible to leave or quit as this will create an impasse which could be problematic and affect your relationships within the practice and client business. You must define an exit strategy that allows partners to walk away or buy each other out, without destroying the business and/or the professional relationship.

Consideration 6: Capital contributions

Work out your capital contributions within the group and what you think you can bring to the group and record it. The contributions must be split between the partners but, most importantly, you must put an equitable value on the contribution of those that cannot raise sufficient capital but do the lion's share of the work or administration. All roles have an intrinsic value in the growth of the business. If someone is able to bring in more money than others but they cannot administrate and run a business, this does not mean that they are a good or bad partner or vice versa. Both skills are essential for the growth of the business.

Situations will change over time. Just look at the recent recession with its length and its numerous dips. Your partnership agreement must be able to reflect and remodel itself based on external factors, which may impact on the profit and equitable split within a partnership.

If you are good at finance then you may consider putting yourself forward to be the compliance officer for finance and administration (COFA) of the partnership. If you are good at administration, you may consider being the compliance officer for legal practice (COLP). You must consider what your individual strengths are and those of the partners you will join or create the partnership with. Too many visionaries as partners will mean the business will have no substance. Too many administrators may mean the partnership is stagnant and may not progress due to a lack of vision.

I advise you to prepare a SWOT analysis of yourself (strengths, weaknesses, opportunities, and threats) and the partnership at the outset. One of the main advantages of a partnership is that you are able to use the skills and the strengths of each individual partner for the whole. What can you bring to the table? What is your USP? If you want to drink champagne then you must bring it to the table. It is of no use turning up wanting champagne if all you are bringing is water!

Consideration 7: 'In pursuit of slow'

Too many people rush into the business idea and a partnership is put together too quickly. It is a business and you must have a business plan. Take your time. Do you think that you will form the partnership and when it is completed the law will have disappeared? Each partner's time, cost and commitment must be clearly understood from the outset before you sign on the dotted line.

Why is it that you pick your fruit in a marketplace better than some people pick partners? You will pick up the fruit, look at it and put it down. Pick up another piece, look at it and put it down. Yet some people go into a partnership without any real thought or understanding of their actual partners or their individual needs. There is nothing worse than finding out that you have chosen the wrong partner, which can affect both your professional and private life. Consider your potential partner's method of doing business, his or her personality and business skills prior to starting the partnership.

Why do we resist slow? Every single invention in the last 100 years has been introduced to allow us to do things quicker – consider the microwave, the washing machine, the car, the train, etc. Although we have more time on our hands, we fill it with other fast things and we do not have enough time for what we really should concentrate on . . . ourselves!

Consideration 8: Integrity

One of the key attributes of a solicitor is integrity. Integrity is key governing the relationship between yourself and your clients, as well as yourself and your partners, and is a responsibility you have to each other and the outside world. You must be asking yourself the following questions:

- Is your trust with your partner(s) based on a real assessment or is it an emotional connection?
- Can you trust the partner(s)?
- How has his or her individual behaviour been in the past?
- Does this person consistently meet his or her commitments (big or small) in both his or her professional and personal life?
- If the partner does half the job, are you prepared to take up the slack?
- Will you resent this?
- Does the partner's other positive attributes outweigh this trait?
- Will the partner do the right thing, legally and professionally especially when it is not convenient or profitable for him or her to do so?

Consideration 9: The five Ds

Always remember the five Ds of partnership (proposed by David Finkel (**www.allbusiness.com/company-activities-management/company-strategy/11480377-1.html**)).

Death

Consider at the outset what will happen if one of the principals of the business or partnership dies. If you are joining an existing partnership, ensure there is a provision for the death of a partner. This could be handled by a buy-sell clause and funded by life insurance for each partner/member.

Disagreement

What happens if you reach an impasse or irreconcilable difference on an issue that is so fundamental to the partnership that it means the partnership cannot continue?

Your agreement must set out how you will handle this and tie it up with a buy-sell agreement as a last resort so that each party can move on and cut their losses if necessary.

Debt

What will happen if any of your partners become insolvent and/or declares bankruptcy? Will you have to take that partner's creditors within your business? Will the insolvent partner's interests revert to the other partners? Make sure the agreement is clear on this point.

Divorce

If a partner gets divorced and, in the divorce settlement, part of his or her interest goes to his or her former spouse, do you really want that individual in your partnership? There must be a contingency within the agreement to cover this point.

Disability

As with most risks that can be covered by insurance, what happens if one of the partners/members becomes incapacitated for any length of time and as a result is not able to contribute his or her time, effort and money to the practice? How will this affect that person's ownership and his or her partnership share and profits, etc.?

Consideration 10: In writing

Get your agreement in writing. Get your agreement in writing. Get your agreement in writing. I can't say any more.

Make sure you agree the terms of your agreement during the honeymoon period and not after when complacency has set in. There will be little wiggle room for negotiation thereafter.

Every partnership, whether a s.1(1) partnership, an LLP or limited company, should be set out in writing and signed by all parties. It is advisable, notwithstanding the fact that you are a lawyer, to have a lawyer look at the agreement. If you are a criminal practitioner, your days of partnership law may be very rusty. Get advice and get it in writing.

What is a s.1(1) partnership?

Section 1(1) of the Partnership Act 1890 defines a partnership as:

> the relation which subsists between persons carrying on a business in common with a view to profit.

Excluded from this definition are:

(a) various forms of companies; and
(b) that legal entity which has become the norm within the legal profession, the LLP, pursuant to the Limited Liability Partnership Act 2000.

A partnership governed by the s.1(1) definition is very different to a company or LLP in that a s.1(1) partnership cannot by itself:

- enter into contracts;
- employ staff to run it; or
- sue or be sued.

The partnership in this sense consists of the partners who comprise the partnership, with no limit on their personal liability for any debts or claims which are incurred by all the partners. If this does not scare you, then read on!

What is an LLP?

It was the threat of litigation and the large awards of damages in alleged negligence claims of the 1980s and 1990s that led to the professions (particularly accountants) to review the nature of the then existing partnerships. This led to the Limited Liability Partnership Act 2000, which came into force on 6 April 2001. This trend towards LLP status was also partly the direct result of the globalisation of legal services, with some foreign law firms already able to operate within the limited liability status regime. Law firms in England and Wales had to change if they wanted to compete globally.

LLPs sit between partnerships and companies, but unlike a partnership, an LLP:

- has a legal personality so it can sue and be sued;
- gives its members the protection of limited liability status;
- much like a company:

    - it must publish annual accounts at Companies House; and
    - it must submit to the regulatory requirements adopted from company law.

LLPs are not based on the partnership form with limited liability as an add on. It is not to be confused with a limited partnership formed under the Limited Partnership Act 1907.

In an LLP there is more flexibility as a member than if you become a partner pursuant to a s.1(1) partnership. An important difference between the two entities is the relationship between the members. If you are a member in an LLP, the relationship may be based on partnership law with the members taxed as partners and not as a corporate body based on company law. The members in an LLP enjoy limited liability. Because of this, the LLP route provides professionals with a greater flexibility and it is not surprising it has become the norm.

Although, there are law firms with full limited company status, we will concentrate in this chapter on the traditional s.1(1) partnerships and LLPs as these entities appear to be more popular. But there are an increasing number of law firms that are now companies, for example:

- Berwins Solicitors – **www.berwin.co.uk**
- Nowell Meller Solicitors – **www.nowellmeller.co.uk**
- Sabretooth Law Limited
- Paragon Law – **www.theparagongroup.co.uk/paragon-law**

Let us look at the differences between these two legal formats for partnerships in more detail.

Table 5.1 The business partnership pursuant to s.1(1) of the Partnership Act 1890 v the LLP pursuant to the Limited Liability Partnership Act 2000

Business partnerships	LLPs
• The business partners personally share responsibility for the business. • All business profits are shared between the partners. • Each partner pays tax on his or her share of the profits.	• Partners have limited personal liability for the debts of the business and liability is limited to their initial investment (unless the veil of incorporation is lifted). • Members may be asked to contribute to the LLPs assets if the member is guilty of misfeasance or his or her actions fall within the special claw-back provisions under the Insolvency Act 1986 if the LLP later goes into liquidation. • Members must contribute by agreement between them. • An LLP requires two members otherwise it becomes a sole practice and personal liability is assumed.
Legal responsibility	
You and your business partners are personally responsible for: • the losses; • items purchased; and • equipment.	There are numerous legal responsibilities which attach as a result of being a director. The key function of the LLP is that it is a body corporate and thus a legal entity separate from its members. It has unlimited capacity and can do almost anything a legal person can do.
How to set up a business partnership	
• The nominated partner registers the partnership with HMRC. • Partners register personally for self-assessment to pay their personal tax and national insurance on their percentage share of the partnership profits. • Complete registration for VAT purposes if applicable.	Partners must incorporate a company at Companies House and notify HMRC when the company starts to trade as a business. Each financial year the partners must: • prepare statutory accounts; and • submit an annual return to Companies House.

Business partnerships	LLPs
Partnership tax liabilities	
The nominated partner must: • submit a partnership tax return; • submit a self-assessment tax return on his or her partnership share per annum. All partners must send in a personal self-assessment tax return per annum; • pay income tax on his or her share of the partnership profits; • pay his or her national insurance; • the partnership will be registered for VAT if receipts exceed the relevant thresholds.	Partners must: • submit a partnership self-assessment tax return to Her Majesty's Revenue and Customs; • register for VAT if applicable; • fill in a personal self-assessment tax return on his or her partnership share per annum. All partners must send in a personal self-assessment tax return per annum; • pay tax and national insurance from his or her share of the partnership profits.

Whichever entity you join or create, it is dangerous to enter into any professional relationship without a written Partnership Agreement and for you to agree your own rules regulating your relationship with each other and the outside world. All forms of partnership have the flexibility for you to:

- agree the partnership share of the profits between the partners/ members;
- confirm responsibility for the management of the partnership/LLP;
- set out the method for making decisions;
- agree when/how new partners/members are appointed or when they are able to retire.

As with a Partnership Agreement pursuant to a s.1(1) partnership, the Member Agreement for an LLP is a private document and confidential to its members and not for public consumption.

The effect of a separate legal entity

An LLP is a body corporate, with legal responsibilities separate from its members as confirmed above. As a result, any change in the LLP's membership does not affect its continued existence, unlike a s.1(1) partnership. In this case, there will be a technical dissolution when one partner leaves or another joins but business does carry on.

Any financial assistance offered to an LLP is often supported by a personal guarantee from its members. Even though the LLP may be treated as a separate legal entity for the purposes of company law and liability, it is treated as a partnership for tax purposes and where credit facilities are given to it. The insolvency regime for an LLP is largely the same as for companies.

There are many other aspects of the law governing partnerships and LLPs but they are too numerous and detailed for us to analyse here. I believe your time and mine would be better spent in outlining the pitfalls that may exist and those you must take into account in your partnership relationships with the outside world and each other.

Before we proceed, however, I would like to touch upon two other forms of partnerships which exist today.

A limited partnership

Definition

A limited partnership is where one or more of the partners is a limited partner who is only liable to the extent of his or her investment. This should not be confused with an LLP, which has more in common with a limited company. A limited partnership is, in almost all other aspects the same as a s.1(1) partnership discussed earlier in this chapter.

Legislation

The provisions for the creation of limited partnerships were introduced by the Limited Partnerships Act 1907, which legislates on those matters pertaining only to limited partnerships. Limited partnerships are otherwise governed by the general partnership legislation, being the Partnership Act 1890.

Differences between a limited partnership and a s.1(1) partnership

The key differences between a limited partnership and a s.1(1) partnership are the following:

- A limited partnership will have at least one general partner who has unlimited liability for the debts and liabilities of the partnership (although a general partner will often be a limited company). The remaining partners' liability for the debts and obligations of the partnership is limited to the amount of their original contributions but they are excluded from the management of the partnership and cannot bind the firm without express permission.
- There is a requirement that a limited partnership is registered at the Register of Companies (Companies House) and the partnership will be deemed a general partnership until so registered.

Alternative business structures (ABSs)

What is an ABS?

An ABS is a firm where a non-lawyer:

- is a manager of the firm; or
- has an ownership-type interest in the firm.

A firm may also be an ABS where another body:

- is a manager of the firm; or
- has an ownership-type interest in the firm;

and at least 10 per cent of that body is controlled by non-lawyers.

A non-lawyer is a person who is not authorised under the Legal Services Act 2007 to carry out reserved legal activities.

ABSs are dealt with in more detail in **Chapter 7**.

Due diligence

The considerations numbered 1 to 10 earlier in the chapter can be adapted for existing and new partnerships but when you are joining an existing partnership, the following due diligence must also be carried out in addition to 1 to 10 above.

The aim of completing your due diligence is to ensure that all the legal and financial issues which relate to the partnership are in order so you are aware of the full picture and can make an informed decision.

Finances

- Ask the partnership for its financial statements, including balance sheets, management accounts, income statements, cash flow forecasts/statements and business tax returns for the past however many years you require.
- Has the firm complied with its SRA obligations in respect of the filing of accounts?
- Obtain copies of the reporting accountant's reports.
- Request proof the partnership is collecting its accounts receivable in a timely manner.
- Does the partnership bill monthly?
- What is the partnership collection time?
- How much bad debt does the partnership write off annually? This may confirm a variation of the figures from what you may be told to what is the reality.

- Is the partnership paying its debts in a timely manner? This will hint at whether the partnership is trading insolvently.
- What are the partnership profit margins per partner?
- Does the partnership have any outstanding mortgages?
- What is the percentage of personally guaranteed debts to LLP debts? The debts of the LLP may not ordinarily attach liability to the partners.
- How much money are you expected to contribute and do you have to add all of your assets?
- Does the partnership employ a full-time financial team?
- Does the partnership have checks and balances to ensure the client account rules are adhered to? Breaches can carry strict liability.

Legal issues

Ask for the professional indemnity history, level of cover, licenses (Financial Conduct Authority), permits and public liability insurance. This will help you decide whether the business is adequately insured. Is the practice involved in any litigation and, if so, what are the potential risks, costs and damages? What are the types of historical claims they have had? Do they set a trend, i.e. lack of supervision in a particular area?

Employees

You were once an employee and therefore you will have copies of the organisational charts, employee handbooks, employment agreements, salary information, benefits, plans and confidentiality agreements, you must request them of the organisation you are joining. You may, however, get a different feel from the partners of how they actually view their staff once you agree to join. This may help you to assess whether any of the existing policies put the business at risk from an HR perspective. Are there any grievances? If the partners'/members' perception is different to that of the staff you may be able to assess whether this is dangerous for the future of the firm as the two perceptions may collide.

Business structure

- Ask for all corporate structure documentation, memorandum and articles of association, partnership agreements and any side agreements, lease of premises, etc.
- Is the business compliant with its SRA obligations and company law?
- Does it have a proper structured growth plan and are there requirements to buy out underperforming partners/members and, if so, at what cost?

Operations

- Ask for a list of the firm's clients, suppliers and vendors.
- Is the client base sufficiently diversified so that the business is not overly reliant on one client?
- Is that client base varying and by what percentage?
- Does the partnership have the necessary equipment and infrastructure in place for its continued growth?

With considerations 1 to 10 earlier in the chapter and my suggested due diligence, I hope you will be in a better position to decide whether or not you want to proceed with a particular partnership or not. It is always better to be safe than sorry! My lists are not exhaustive, but I hope you will agree they provide some practical assistance.

Regulation

I want to make it clear that the above lists set out the due diligence and considerations that I would expect you to address before you enter into an existing partnership or create a new one. They do not cover all the regulations and obligations which are imposed by the SRA's Code of Conduct and authorisation requirements. I have assumed that you will look these up yourself on the SRA website and view the following:

- The Practice Framework Rules, which govern who you should be in partnership with, **www.sra.org.uk/solicitors/handbook/practising/content.page**.
- The Authorisation Rules, which govern the body corporate itself and the conditions of authorisation, i.e. COFA and COLP, **www.sra.org.uk/solicitors/handbook/authorisationrules**.
- The Practising Regulations, which relate to the rules and regulations governing practising certificates, **www.sra.org.uk/solicitors/handbook/practisingregulations/content.page**.

To summarise, I would respectively suggest to you that when you consider whether you wish to enter into a partnership or not, you consider the following:

(a) What type of partnership do you want to go into or create? The main emphasis will be on liability.
(b) Ask your questions of your prospective partners and existing partners very early on in your negotiations and be as honest and truthful as possible.
(c) Conduct your due diligence and ask those difficult questions. If your partners are not prepared to give you the information you request now, what else will they be hiding when you join?

(d) Make sure that whatever you enter into or create, it is compliant with the SRA rules and regulations, some of which are listed above.

The route to partnership is not paved with gold and I hope I have given you some food for thought so that you can avoid any potholes!

Chapter 6

Setting up a law firm

Tony Roe

Setting up my own law firm was not something I had nurtured for years, nor indeed, what I had ever imagined that I might do. However, back in 2007, when my (then) firm announced that my area of law was not part of future plans, it was suggested to me that I might start my own practice. That is what I did the following year.

This chapter must be put in context. It is a personal view based on my own experience. I am a family law solicitor, pure and simple. I am not qualified to talk about the best sort of business structures to adopt or advise on regulatory matters. I am certainly not an accountant. This chapter does not set out to be in any way authoritative or comprehensive. It simply offers a few vignettes. If any tips prove useful, I am pleased.

Moreover, anything I might have to say is put in the shade by Martin Smith's *Setting Up and Managing a Legal Practice* (4th edition, Law Society, 2012). I searched around for some helpful information for a long time before chancing upon this book. It was probably the best investment I made. It also makes very good management reading even for those not wanting to set up their own outfit.

The Law Society's *Small Legal Business Toolkit* is aimed at sole practices, small firms and solicitors thinking of setting up in business. Published in September 2008, it is a little out of date but is free to download at **www.lawmanagementsection.org.uk/pages/news/item/289**.

Why set up a new law firm at all?

Setting up your own law firm enables you to design your own practice just as you would want it to be. You are your own boss. You can create a bespoke business in a dynamic and rapidly changing market. You become less of a lawyer and more of an entrepreneur.

The financial downturn had not hit when I opened up shop in February 2008. I may not have been so keen to do so under present conditions, particularly in the light of the economy and the relatively new regulatory system.

Five years ago, the Solicitors Regulation Authority (SRA) told me that, as a solicitor qualified to supervise, all I needed to do was to have the firm registered and to get insurance. Each of these elements is now much more complex and more costly.

Even though you may be 'qualified to supervise' under rule 12 of the SRA Practice Framework Rules 2011, it is well worth finding a good course to refresh your own management skills. At the very least you should read the SRA Handbook from cover to cover (covered in more detail below). The handbook is being continually revised so refer to the SRA website for the most up-to-date version: **http://sra.org.uk/solicitors/handbook**. Moreover, the Law Society regularly publishes helpful practice notes which are required reading for any solicitor, particularly those contemplating creating a new practice. These are available at **www.lawsociety.org.uk/advice/practice-notes**.

You must examine very carefully why you want to start a new firm. If you have the idea that it might be a lucrative thing to do, forget it.

Getting in and getting out

It might seem odd to talk about getting out of a firm that is yet to be set up, but this is a key issue. Running a law firm is not a hobby. One cannot dip in and out of it. It demands full-time attention and commitment and brings with it its own stresses and rewards.

Arguably, it is harder to get out of your own firm than it is to set it up. Retirement and succession issues should be addressed and planned for in good time. One of the major drivers of this is the significant cost of 'run-off' professional indemnity insurance. This can cost many times the annual premium, supposedly to cover any potential claims following the winding up of the business.

The Law Society publishes a handy practice note on this topic entitled Closing down your practice: regulatory requirements, which is available at **www.lawsociety.org.uk/advice/practice-notes/closing-down-your-practice**.

The groundwork

There are plenty of professionals who may offer to help plan and set up your new practice. Of course individual experts will be needed along the way, however I would suggest that there is little point in your venture unless you 'own' it. If you do not, you might as well buy someone else's firm, an unknown quantity with plenty of potential risks.

The beauty about setting up afresh is that it can be planned from the ground up. There is no historic baggage.

Outcomes-focused regulation

Outcomes-focused regulation (OFR) was introduced by the SRA on 6 October 2011. OFR applies to all those the SRA regulates, including ABSs, which were introduced at the same time.

The SRA says that OFR focuses on the high-level principles and outcomes that should drive the provision of legal services for consumers. It replaced a detailed and prescriptive rulebook with a targeted, risk-based approach concentrating on the standards of service to consumers. The SRA adds that there is greater flexibility for firms in how they achieve outcomes (standards of service) for clients. It is certainly not a 'light-touch' system.

The SRA Handbook

The SRA Handbook brings together all of the regulatory requirements that apply to all those it regulates, as listed below.

Principles

There are 10 Principles. These stand alone at the beginning of the handbook and underpin all the SRA's regulatory requirements. Principles 1–6 are similar to the Solicitors' Code of Conduct 2007 core duties. The new Principles 7–10 relate to the management of a practice and compliance with regulatory arrangements. New requirements include those to 'treat clients fairly', those relating to business management and Chapter 7 of the SRA Code of Conduct 2011, as well as those on outsourcing.

Code of Conduct

The Code of Conduct has outcomes-focused provisions, which show how the Principles apply in practice to conduct matters and provide clarity for consumers (we call them clients) about the outcomes and protections they can expect. The Code comprises mandatory outcomes and non-mandatory indicative behaviours.

Outcomes (O)

These describe what is expected to be achieved to comply with the Principles in specific contexts, as set out in the different chapters in the Code. The outcomes are mandatory.

Indicative behaviours (IB)

These provide non-mandatory examples of the kind of behaviours which may establish whether the relevant outcomes and the Principles have been complied with.

Accounts Rules

These are rules for protection of client money, including outcomes-focused provisions on authorising withdrawals from the client account and accounting for interest.

Authorisation and Practising Requirements

The Authorisation and Practising Requirements are the approach to authorisation, appointing compliance officers, notification requirements and admission and education requirements.

Client Protection

Outcomes and rules in relation to indemnity insurance and the Compensation Fund.

Discipline and Costs Recovery

The approach to fining and disciplining firms and individuals.

Specialist Services

Provisions on financial services, property selling and European cross-border activities.

Glossary

Definitions for the whole handbook.

The fact that, according to *Managing Partner* magazine, quoting the SRA's own figures, two-thirds of law firms say that OFR takes more time than the previous system of regulation means that getting the groundwork right from the start is crucial. Existing firms are advised to carry out a comprehensive compliance review which should result in a risk register and a plan to address any non-compliance. A new firm can, and indeed must, get it right from the start.

The Code of Conduct requires any firm or entity to have certain effective systems in place including, for example, budget control, recording conflicts of interests and methods of supervision. Any firm should have conducted a risk assessment, taking into account the size and complexity of the firm, its work and areas of risk.

The SRA may enquire how an outcome is being met if the IBs are not followed. It would be wise to record how this is to be done. Documentation is key to practical OFR even though its emphasis is not apparently on this. This sort of record may form part of the office manual.

Compliance officers

All recognised and licensed bodies must nominate two types of compliance officer: a compliance officer for legal practice (COLP) and a compliance officer for finance and administration (COFA).

COLPs are responsible for taking all reasonable steps to:

- ensure that the authorised body complies with all terms and conditions of its authorisation, save any obligations imposed under the SRA Accounts Rules;
- ensure that the authorised body complies with relevant statutory obligations;
- record any failure to comply with authorisation or statutory obligations and make such records available to the SRA.

COLPs must report any material failure to the SRA as soon as reasonably practicable.

COFAs must:

- take all reasonable steps to ensure that the authorised body, its employees and managers comply with any obligations imposed under the SRA Accounts Rules;
- keep a record of any failure to comply and make this record available to the SRA;
- report any material failure (either taken on its own or as part of a pattern of failures) to the SRA as soon as reasonably practicable.

A COLP must be a lawyer of England and Wales, a registered European lawyer or an individual registered with the Bar Standards Board under reg.17 of the European Communities (Lawyer's Practice) Regulations 2000 (SI 2000/1119) and who is:

- a manager or employee of the authorised body;
- designated as its COLP and whose designation is approved by the SRA; and
- of sufficient seniority and in a position of sufficient responsibility to fulfil the role.

A COFA need not be a lawyer. The COFA may be a manager or employee of the authorised body who is:

- designated as its COFA and whose designation is approved by the SRA; and
- of sufficient seniority and in a position of sufficient responsibility to fulfil the role.

Clearly COLPs and COFAs will need access to management systems and other relevant information such as client files and business information.

A recognised sole practitioner, like any other entity, needs a COLP and a COFA (reg.4.8 of the SRA Practising Regulations 2011) and, indeed, a sole practitioner can be both.

The Law Society has published two practical toolkits to help practitioners get to grips with the roles of COLPs and COFAs (*COLPs Toolkit* (Law Society, 2012); *COFAs Toolkit* (Law Society, 2012)).

Authorisation

Only those individuals and firms meeting the SRA's criteria for authorisation or approval (including the requirements to be suitable and capable of providing legal services to the required standard) are authorised or approved. An overview of the authorisation process, as well as forms and guidance, are available on the SRA website.

Office manual

There is no absolute need for a firm to have an office manual. However, the SRA's own materials show an example of dealing with one particular firm and state that the firm's office manual demonstrated its systems and controls, including provision for the effective management.

The SRA requires a practice's staff to be appropriately trained in compliance issues, including the roles of the COLP and COFA. The firm must also clearly communicate its policies to its staff, which is another possible use for an office manual.

Business plan

The business plan can form the basis of a firm's office manual. It should not be seen as a one-off but a living document which should be revisited regularly. Professional indemnity insurers regularly ask that a firm's business plan, along with a CV, accompanies its insurance proposal even several years after the firm was founded.

There are many approaches to writing a business plan. As a template, I used one included in *Setting Up and Managing a Legal Practice* mentioned above. I got to the thirteenth version of my plan before finding a management accountant to run it by. I then showed it to another accountant before I gave it to various banks I approached.

A number of the bigger professional indemnity insurers make suggested plans available to clients. Joining the Law Society's Law Management Section can be worthwhile as it provides very useful information including suggestions for inclusion in a business plan (**www.lawmanagement section.org.uk**). The Law Society's Small Firms Division is also a valuable community for small practices (**www.lawsociety.org.uk/smallfirms**).

Your business plan should include budgets. Be honest and do not overstate the firm's aspirations, even though one might want to impress the bank.

Funding

Bankers say that the cheapest form of funding is to use one's own finance rather than to borrow someone else's. Trite, perhaps, but accurate nevertheless. Even if you are in the fortunate position of not having to borrow, any bank will still want to know that the firm will be sound enough before it will offer its facilities.

Where your own resources do not allow, friends or family may be worth approaching before you start commercial borrowing.

If there is a need to borrow, how much is needed? This is probably the most common question I am asked. The answer is that it depends. The only accurate way of measuring is to prepare a budget. No budget is ever going to be totally accurate, however a decent stab at figures will go a long way.

What sort of firm will it be?

Know your own firm. Every discipline and client profile base is different. When I was setting up, I had in mind that a virtual firm might be the way forward as well as avoiding the need for costly premises. It was put to me that in my area of divorce and family law, with my prospective client base being higher net worth individuals, these clients would expect me to have a 'proper' office. Moreover, it is not very easy to see a matrimonial client in his or her own home, especially when that client is at odds with his or her spouse still residing there.

In other cases, you might have a practice that you can run from home. Meeting clients there may or may not be desirable. It could also throw up security and insurance issues. In any event, check the terms of any domestic lease or mortgage conditions to ensure that nothing obstructs running a business from home.

Serviced offices offer highly flexible arrangements. These can extend from hiring a meeting room for an hour or two to fully serviced arrangements with telephone answering and a reception.

I took a longer term view and decided to rent office space from the start, however I still recall the sinking feeling when I signed up for a three-year term, knowing that I had just become liable for a significant rent, even before client fees had started coming in.

If you are contemplating entering into a lease, take professional valuation advice as to the level of the rent and any rent-free period you may be able to negotiate. Take legal advice as to the terms of the lease and any break clauses it may contain.

Main expenditure

Professional indemnity insurance (PII)

PII is likely to be one of the most significant expenses. Although it is a labour intensive process, it is worth approaching more than one provider. A good step is to contact a reputable broker whose services can prove invaluable. I have come across cases of one insurer looking to charge a premium twice that of another so it pays to shop around.

At the outset, I found it reasonably convenient and helpful to approach the insurer of the firm where I had been a partner for some 10 years. The insurer knew me and was also aware that I had not been responsible for any claims.

The Law Society publishes helpful information relating to PII. The *Gazette* also often carries relevant supplements as the renewal season approaches.

IT

IT hardware is only as good as its warranty and any IT professional who might support it. Some may prefer to rent or lease and have built-in support contracts. The kit is not going to last forever so budget to renew the equipment within three years.

Cloud computing has come a long way in a short space of time and is worth considering for your practice. Of course it is imperative that you have a secure system. Many smartphones used by solicitors feature cloud technology even though the same solicitors might be suspicious of running their office systems on it.

Searching for the right accounts package, office and case-management software can be a daunting task. Your budget may be a key consideration, as may scalability. Getting a software firm to demonstrate a package to you is a must. Speaking to lawyers in other firms about their systems can also be extremely helpful.

Furniture, supplies, etc.

Office furniture is pricey when new but, as large organisations regularly renew it, good quality used items can be found on the market.

I soon found out that using a stationery supplier to deliver personally was very expensive. It worked out much cheaper, and almost as quick, to order online. Registering to become a member of a local cash and carry might prove economical.

Location

If the firm is to have a non-home based office, where should it be? This requires a good personal knowledge of the proposed area to check its appropriateness for the desired type of work to be offered. In the absence of that, good market research is needed.

The input of a surveyor or valuer can be useful, offering a professional opinion on the commercial profile of the possible location.

What sort of structure will the firm have?

In 2012, SRA figures showed that, since October 2009, the number of sole practitioner firms in England and Wales dropped from 4,095 to 3,377. Partnership numbers fell 26 per cent to 2,896. The number of incorporated companies almost doubled in the three years to 2,980. Limited liability partnerships rose to 1,541.

The structure not in these figures is the ABS, only recently introduced. By January 2013, 75 of these had been licensed, big and small. One reason for some applications was to have non-lawyers as co-owners, a model which can include family members. (See **Chapters 5** and **7** for more information on the different structures available.)

What sort of work will the firm do?

Do what you know. Resist any hankering to branch out into an area of law of which you have had no experience. With the SRA's attention on risk assessment and overall supervision of the firm, practising your own field of law is common sense.

Finance

As part of the planning stage, involve an accountant. Make sure that he or she has experience in carrying out SRA audits.

Do not try to deal with the bookkeeping and any VAT returns yourself. Get a good legal cashier with up-to-date SRA training to do it for you.

VAT

Take professional advice about registering for VAT in the light of prevailing thresholds, your turnover and likely expenses.

Marketing

Very early on I was advised to tell anyone and everyone that I was setting up a law firm. Actually telling someone helps the project take shape in your mind. With the word out there, you cannot let them down and this means you have to go through with the idea.

It may come as some surprise to you but many clients will give a new business a try.

Senior professionals have told me that, when they were starting their business, they went to the 'opening of an envelope'. This is not bad advice and I found that, when out in the bazaars, business folk were genuinely interested in my story. Indeed, I was taken aback by the support that I got from others, including from rival lawyers. I learnt a lot from their stories too.

You should prepare a marketing plan building on successful past ideas. Remember that advertising is only one part of marketing, and a costly one at that. Build marketing costs into the overall planned budget.

Many marketing initiatives come without cost. Social media is a particular example. Lawyers seem to either love it or live in fear of it. Setting up Twitter, Facebook and LinkedIn accounts all come free. Local newspapers want to fill up blank space and may use relevant, reliable and timely copy, as long as there is a local angle. Simple websites are relatively cheap to set up. Learn how to make yours as effective as possible.

Cashflow and financial management

On 15 March 2013 at the Law Society risk and compliance conference, SRA Executive Director, Samantha Barrass, said:

> The financial failure of Cobbetts has served as a wake-up to call to the legal services sector, where the risk of financial collapse is more acute than ever.

Ms Barrass went on to say:

> There are some worrying practices that we are encountering in our supervision of the sector, and can be seen as critical indicators of financial instability.

These practices to be avoided include:

- payments made to partners irrespective of 'cash in the bank';
- all net profits drawn with no reserve pot retained;
- short-term borrowings to fund partners' tax;
- VAT received used as cash received, resulting in further borrowings to fund VAT due to HMRC;
- partners out of touch with office account bank balances;
- heavy dependence on high overdraft borrowings; and
- partners' capital injection is 100 per cent borrowed.

Having good cash flow is probably the most important financial strategy to have. Regular billing and prompt cash collection can make the difference between success and bankruptcy.

Data protection

The Data Protection Act 1998 requires every data controller who is processing personal information to register with the Information Commissioner's Office (ICO), unless they are exempt. A payment of £35 a year is all it costs. Simply arrange a direct debit so you don't fall foul of annual requirements.

Holidays and work/life balance

Running a law firm may be a vocation for some. In reality it is a business like any other; one works to live, not the other way around.

At the outset, assume that the enterprise will require you to work long hours, seven days a week. This pattern may last for a number of months but is not sustainable in the medium or long term. Ultimately, the time needed by the firm will depend on its clients, its management and the aspirations you may have for it.

The SRA states at IB(7.4) that 'making arrangements for the continuation of your firm in the event of absences and emergencies, for example holiday or sick leave, with the minimum interruption to clients' business' would be compliant with its requirements.

The Law Society's practice note on supervision says that this may include ensuring that there is another person who is 'qualified to supervise' in your practice. It says sole practitioners should have an arrangement with another solicitor to supervise your practice until you return from any absence. This could be a locum or a mutual arrangement with another local solicitor.

Ill health and death

There must be continuing management of a practice in the event of incapacity. A power of attorney, appointing a solicitor, enables you to choose who might manage your affairs should you no longer have the ability to do so.

Insurance must be put in place to protect the practice in the unfortunate event of anything happening to you. A 'Keyman' policy is designed to pay out an agreed cash sum if a key individual ceases work due to death or critical ill health. Separate private health cover might speed up treatment, as well as providing regular health checks. A good insurance broker can help you look at the options and costings.

Make a will if you have not already done so. The Sole Practitioners Group (SPG) has clauses on its website to be included in a will of a sole practitioner solicitor appointing a special executor. It suggests that one should consult a solicitor who is a member of the Society of Trust and Estate Practitioners.

Emergency planning

Making arrangements for eventualities forms part of managing your practice. As mentioned above, IB(7.4) refers to 'making arrangements for the continuation of your firm in the event of . . . emergencies'. This may cover making provisions for fire or flood or simply IT failure. Ken Seaken's article on contingency planning is useful on this topic, available on the SPG website at **www.spg.uk.com/knowhow/continuity/contingency planning. doc**.

Support

Running a small practice can be a lonely business. It can be a great help to join informal networks, local professional groups or simply talk to someone who has been in the same position.

Conclusion

Don't try to be an expert in every discipline needed to help you set up a new practice. Invest in the professional skills of others, whether they are accountants, solicitors or surveyors. Surround yourself with this 'cabal of sages' and this will ease the pressure on you.

If you are thinking of setting up your own firm, I hope something in this chapter has been of some help. Good luck.

Chapter 7

Further options

Melissa Hardee, Steven Durno and Leslie Moran

Part A: Working in 'new business vehicles' – *Melissa Hardee*

The legal profession has always been seen as overly traditional and rooted in the past. This is no longer the case, following the Legal Services Act 2007 (LSA), the licensing of Alternative Business Structures (ABSs) and general quantum leaps in technology. So, what does that mean for career and job options?

What is an ABS?

The first thing to say is that just because an organisation is licensed as an ABS, it does not necessarily guarantee that it will be intrinsically different to a traditional law firm. It really depends on what makes the organisation an ABS. An ABS, after all, is just another vehicle for delivering legal services, in the same way that firms traditionally have been partnerships or, more recently, limited liability partnerships (LLPs).

 The reasons an organisation may decide to become licensed as an ABS can be many and varied, including:

- to have someone who is not a solicitor as a 'manager' ('partner' in non-LSA speak);
- the fact that the ABS is owned externally or has external investors;
- to provide non-legal as well as legal services; or
- the company is an established brand that has diversified into legal services in addition to its core business activities.

The law firm ABS

In the traditional type of firm which has become an ABS because it has made, say, its finance director a partner (or 'manager' in LSA-speak), solicitors will probably have much the same role as in non-ABS firms. The firm may or may not use paralegals, and it may have developed more innovative ways of delivering its legal services, which we will come on to below, but in terms of job opportunities and career paths, it is likely to be the same as in a non-ABS firm. What it does mean though for paralegals is that there may be a career path in an ABS firm which is not available to them in

73

non-ABS firms, if the firm is prepared (or has been on at least one occasion) to make a non-solicitor a manager.

Having said all that, innovation in the delivery of legal services in the current market is coming largely from new entrants and new forms of ABSs. What has given rise to all this innovation is essentially a downward pressure on costs – the need of the consumer to have affordable legal services – at the same time that legal services have been liberalised by the LSA. You are seeing this with new ownership structures, new service models and with established brands entering the market diversifying into legal services. This opens up all sorts of opportunities for solicitors, as well as giving rise to the need for new skills and expertise for these new roles.

The corporate ABS

For instance, in a corporate ABS, the ABS is likely to be run as a business first and a legal practice second (assuming legal services are its main business, which it may not be). For the solicitor working in a corporate ABS, one difference they will notice immediately from the traditional law firm partnership is that of centralised, and fast, decision-making. Working as a solicitor in a corporate ABS may be very similar in terms of role to working in a non-ABS law firm. It is a different environment, however, and what will also be required in addition to legal knowledge and skills is a business focus: commercial awareness, a focus on delivering services and managing and meeting customer needs. Entrepreneurship is also likely to be highly valued as well as an ability to think outside the box and in a commercial context. Although firms increasingly require commercial awareness (an understanding of the law firm as a business), they still tend to be lawyers first and businessmen second. Where the ABS is owned by, say, a private equity company that will be looking for a return on its investment, then an understanding of the business imperative will be very important, as will the need for management skills. Equally, solicitors who work for a corporate ABS will have corporate career paths open to them, in the same way as those involved in the company's sales, product management, research and technology, information technology and so on do. It is in fact not dissimilar to that of the in-house corporate lawyer.

Commoditisation of legal services

The commoditisation of legal services provides one example of new ways of working as a solicitor. Commoditisation proceeds on the basis that a lot of what solicitors do is process-based rather than bespoke and therefore can be standardised, systematised, packaged and commoditised – 'process re-engineering' by another name, or 'de-composing' as it is also, rather un-fragrantly, referred to! This comes from the manufacturing model and the idea of delivering large volumes at lower prices through economies of scale. What it has generally turned out to mean in the delivery of legal services is deployment of large numbers of paralegals, and far fewer qualified solicitors, for process-based work such as conveyancing, personal injury claims, and the like. However, these paralegals need to be supervised, particularly if the firm or ABS (a firm does not need to be an ABS to offer commoditised legal services or to employ large numbers of paralegals) is regulated by the SRA. If so, a solicitor working in that sort of organisation will have a supervisory role in terms of ensuring the quality of the work and that there is no unauthorised practice of law by non-qualified persons. Think of the supervisor of a production line in a biscuit factory, tasting the sample biscuit as it goes down the line, rather than making the actual biscuits.

Outsourcing

An extension of the trend to commoditise legal services is to outsource those services wholly or in part. Depending on how this is done – the terms 'off-shoring', 'near-shoring', 'at home working', 'sub-contracting', etc. spring to mind – outsourcing provides opportunity for more flexible and independent working. Continuing the manufacturing analogy, however, it is more like 'piece-working', rather than being part of the manufacturing process from start to finish. So, the solicitor may be the 'piece-worker', or, as discussed above, he or she may be supervising a number of paralegal 'piece-workers'.

This sort of supervisory role is not dissimilar to being a 'trainee supervisor' in a firm, although in a firm one tends to supervise only one trainee at a time, rather than many paralegals. Being able to identify problems and troubleshoot appropriately are therefore important skills to have in this sort of supervisory role. The other issue though is just how much of the legal work will there be for you as a solicitor to do in addition to supervising? In other words, are you more supervisor than practitioner?

Technology-based delivery of legal services

Another innovation in legal services, not confined to ABSs, that opens up different types of jobs for solicitors is in technology-based delivery of legal services. Given that we all buy pretty much anything online these days, do our banking online and book our holidays online, it seems a no-brainer that legal services are delivered online or over the phone. In the simplest form of technology-based delivery, the consumer can access a template to produce the legal document they need, underpinned by automated document assembly software. I say 'consumer' quite deliberately, as in this 'DIY' model, the consumer does not in fact become a client. Although the solicitor does not figure in the process as such, where the solicitor does have a role is in the development of the document templates and questionnaires which are available to consumers to 'draft' the legal document they need. For the solicitor who is into technology, doing a back-room role which is akin to that of some professional support lawyer-type roles may appeal.

Then there is the 'do it with me' option. The consumer (again, the relationship may not be enough to turn them into a client) works with a solicitor online to produce the document the consumer needs. In this, the solicitor has an active role, just not in person. In fact, the solicitor is unlikely ever to meet a consumer using any of these online services.

There is also the telephone call line. This usually involves a non-solicitor taking the call from a potential client and carrying out the initial triage so that the call can be referred to the appropriate lawyer – or non-lawyer for that matter (see the discussion of commoditised services above). Providing legal services over the telephone requires good listening and interviewing skills – all things a solicitor is trained to do – so that the solicitor can obtain the information needed to provide the necessary service. However, unlike using listening and interviewing skills in person, over the phone you are speaking to someone you have never met and whose body language and other signals you cannot see. If you have good telephone skills, then this should not be a problem, and it may have the advantage of taking you out of the office environment, if that is a plus for you (although potentially into a call centre environment depending on how the call line is set up). If you thrive on personal contact with the client and developing the client relationship, however, then technology-based services may not appeal. This also goes for the online 'do it with me' type of service delivery, and, at the extreme end of the technology-based delivery spectrum, the virtual law firm.

Virtual law firms

In a virtual law firm you are still working as a solicitor, just over the ether. The big advantage of virtual law firms and online delivery is that of flexibility and independence: you do not need to be in an office to do your job, you don't even need to work five days a week, all day, every day – provided that you are responsive and meet the client's expectations and deliver what you have promised. The big driver for this type of service delivery is being able to deliver the legal services the client needs more quickly and efficiently – and more cost effectively – than traditional law firms are able to do. So, if a better work/life balance is what you are after, then technology-based delivery may be for you. However, be aware that working in this way requires very strong personal organisational skills, and self-discipline, to manage your workload, delivery targets and your business.

76

Going freelance

The freelance model is closely related to the virtual firm. Lawyers are inherently risk-averse, traditional creatures. However, if you do crave better quality of life, are not fussed about a career path to partnership, are prepared to be brave, but not so brave as to want to set up your own firm, then working as a freelance lawyer, either for a network of lawyers or for one of the new legal resourcing businesses, may be for you. A word of warning, depending on how the business works, you may need to have a portable practice, ideally with clients who will follow you rather than the firm. Depending on how you deliver your legal services (i.e. face-to-face or electronically), you may encounter the same issues described above in relation to online delivery. You may never meet your client or, if you do and you have been parachuted in, you won't be building an ongoing relationship with the client, just as it is for locum lawyers. You won't be part of a team and won't necessarily have the support that you probably take for granted within a firm – secretarial support, training, access to other expertise in the firm and being part of a community. If you are a social animal who likes to work with people and have people around them, then this way of working may not be for you.

So, the point is to be honest with yourself about how and where you would like to work, but also how in fact you are best able to work (there is a difference!) and also whether you have the self-discipline and organisational and management skills to work alone effectively. If you do, then there are all sorts of possibilities opening up for you in the new legal services market.

Working with other 'lawyers'

One other thing to mention about ABSs is that it works both ways and that solicitors could go into business with one or other of the 'authorised persons' under the LSA, namely, barristers, licensed conveyancers, chartered legal executives, patent attorneys, trade mark agents, legal costs draftsmen, or notaries – subject to being permitted to do so by the relevant regulator. Further, solicitors may work in an ABS that is licensed by a licensing authority other than the SRA (not all ABSs have to be or are licensed by the SRA, the Council of Licensed Conveyancers being a notable alternative). The SRA would retain jurisdiction over you as a solicitor for matters of professional misconduct, but for all other purposes, your delivery of legal services within the ABS would be regulated by the ABS's chosen regulator. Just a thought.

Part B: Solicitor advocates and the judiciary – *Steven Durno*

Solicitor advocates

As a student on the Legal Practice Course you will have received some tuition on advocacy skills. Many solicitors will never appear in court themselves but for some that taste is enough to persuade future solicitors that their professional life lies in advocacy. Other solicitors become advocates as an adjunct to their practices. If you become a criminal practitioner, advocacy will form the basis of your career. So how do you become a solicitor advocate?

When you are admitted as a solicitor you will have rights of audience in the magistrates' court and the county court (though that position will change once the Quality Assurance Scheme for Advocates (QASA) is implemented). Historically, rights of audience in the higher courts were exclusive to barristers. The first break with that tradition occurred in 1972 when solicitors appearing for defendants in the magistrates' court were permitted to appear in the Crown Court on any appeal or committal for sentencing. The Courts and Legal Services Act 1990 finally ended barristers' monopoly of rights of audience in the higher courts. The Law Society as an authorised body for the purpose of rights of audience became entitled to grant rights of audience to solicitors. To access higher rights of audience you will have to comply with additional assessment requirements and be accredited by the SRA.

You can attain higher rights in the criminal or civil courts. Over 3,000 solicitors hold higher rights in the criminal courts, over 900 in the civil courts and over 1,300 in all courts. To be able to apply for higher rights of audience you must pass an advocacy assessment based on competency standards prescribed by the SRA. You will be assessed by an organisation which has been authorised by the SRA. You will be tested on your understanding of court procedures, evidence and ethics. You will be required to undertake a case study or to participate in a court room simulation exercise. You will find full details of the application process on the SRA's website at **www.sra.org.uk/solicitors/accreditation/higher-rights-of-audience.page**.

Looking into the future, all criminal advocates, whatever their professional background, will be required to be authorised to appear in court as an advocate under QASA. The Scheme has been formulated at the behest of the Legal Services Board by a Joint Advocacy Group comprising the SRA, the Bar Standards Board and ILEX Professional Standards. It is based on prescribed competency standards against which all advocates will be assessed. For you to appear in the magistrates' court you will need to register with the SRA and undertake 15 hours of assessed advocacy continuing professional development (CPD) each year. At the end of five years you will need to re-register with the SRA. If you have not been appearing in the magistrates' court as an advocate, you will lose your right to appear in the magistrates' court at the end of five years.

Once you have gained experience of criminal advocacy in the magistrates' court you can apply for rights of audience in the higher courts. You will be required to register with the SRA and in the next two years obtain judicial evaluation of your performance in the Crown Court from the judges in your first two cases. Again after five years you will need to re-apply to the SRA. If you do not undertake cases before a jury, as is the case with about half of solicitor advocates, and are a 'plea only advocate', you can apply for rights in the Crown Court and will be required to attend an assessment centre. Once again authorisation will run for five years.

QASA is framed around the grading of cases between one of four levels. Cases in the magistrates' court will be at Level 1 and the most serious offences at Level 4. Once you have gained experience in the Crown Court you can apply to graduate from Level 2 to Level 3 by undergoing the same process of authorisation. QASA will be rolled out circuit by circuit with advocates practising on the Midland and Western Circuits being required to apply for authorisation from the end of September 2013.

In the past the best solicitor advocates learnt by sitting behind more experienced advocates to see their craft in action. With the decline in income from legal aid fees, that is no longer an affordable luxury. You will have to learn advocacy skills on the job and through any training that you can gain. The Law Society has established an Advocacy Section, the primary purpose of which is to assist its members in honing their advocacy skills. The Section offers training courses and webinars. You can find details at **www.lawsociety.org.uk/communities/advocacy**. The Solicitors Association of Higher Court Advocates offers similar training opportunities for its members (see **www.sahca.org.uk**).

At the outset of your career as a solicitor you will not have the depth of knowledge of advocacy enjoyed by a newly qualified barrister. After all advocacy skills form the bulk of their training prior to being called to the bar and while in pupillage. With experience though, you will become every bit as qualified to appear in the courts as any barrister. Today there are many outstanding solicitor advocates. Nearly all cases in the magistrates' court and the youth court are now undertaken by solicitor advocates. As a result competition between solicitor advocates and barristers continues to intensify, particularly in the context of reductions in legal aid fees and the prospect of price competitive tendering for legal aid contracts. The days of healthy incomes from criminal practice have passed. If you want to become a criminal advocate in future you will need to be wholly committed to your trade.

The judiciary

The age of austerity and the consequent reduction in the opportunities available within the legal professions have led many solicitors to reassess their career prospects. One option which has attracted increased interest is applying for a judicial appointment. The number of applications for each vacant post has risen significantly.

Many barristers embark on their careers with a clear strategic goal – pupillage, a place in chambers, junior, silk, judge. It is rare for a solicitor to hold similar aspirations for a place on the bench. Nonetheless, solicitors ought to include consideration of the possibility of a judicial appointment from the outset of their careers. Whether keeping the option at the back of the mind or deliberately setting out with that as a long-term goal, it is never too late to start to build a career portfolio which will enhance your chances of success.

Since 2006 judicial appointments have been the responsibility of the Judicial Appointments Commission (JAC) which operates a fair and open recruitment process independent from the government. The JAC runs the selection exercises for each post and then submits recommendations for appointment to the Lord Chancellor or the Lord Chief Justice depending on the seniority of the post. The JAC is under a statutory duty to recommend appointments solely on merit – the old days of the tap on the shoulder have long gone, together with the bias in favour of the appointment of white male barristers from Oxbridge.

The Tribunals, Courts and Enforcement Act 2007 reduced the statutory eligibility for judicial appointment from either seven or 10 years since admission to the acquisition of five or seven years' post-qualification legal experience depending on the specific judicial post. Each autumn those solicitors attaining that level of experience receive a letter from the Minister for Justice and the President of the Law Society advising them that they are now eligible for judicial appointment. The application packs for individual selection exercises will specify exactly what other experience may be required. For example, the Lord Chancellor expects lawyers appointed to full-time judicial to have at least two years' experience sitting as a part-time fee paid judge. It is exceptional for a lawyer to be appointed straight to a full-time salaried post.

There is no formal career structure for judges. However, it is possible to progress from one level of appointment to another. For example, a person starting out as a fee paid deputy district judge or tribunal judge could reasonably expect to gain a salaried appointment at that level and could progress to the circuit bench. The other main point of entry is to become a recorder and they graduate either to the circuit bench or the High Court. Progression is by way of application in advertised selection exercises.

Details of current selection exercises can be found on both the JAC and the Law Society websites. Those interested in applying for a judicial office can register via the JAC's website at **www.judicialappointments.gov.uk** to receive its electronic newsletter and to be notified when a selection exercise in which they would like to participate is launched. That website carries a considerable amount of information about the selection process including examples of written tests which have been used previously. The JAC organises regular road shows in conjunction with the Law Society for those considering applying for judicial office. They are advertised through Professional Update and the website with places booked via the website.

The JAC also runs the selection exercises for appointment to the various tribunals within the HM Courts & Tribunals Service. The majority of the tribunals judiciary are drawn from the pool of practising solicitors, so it is well worth considering a post on one of the tribunals as a starting point and as a means of gaining judicial experience. High Court Judge Mr Justice Hickinbottom famously started his career as a parking adjudicator. The skills of solicitors engaged in mediation, arbitration and dispute resolution may well be applicable to the work of a tribunal judge.

Part-time salaried working is possible at all levels below the High Court and has proved very popular with both new applicants and established judges. As a fee paid judge (and two years service at this level is normally a pre-requisite for a salaried appointment) you will be able to arrange to sit to suit your convenience. The requirement is a minimum of 15 days per year which will be agreed in advance. That minimum requirement includes time for judicial training organised by the Judicial College both for those newly appointed and thereafter on an ongoing basis. It is not necessary to give up the day job in order to become a judge if sitting in a fee paid capacity. Once appointed to a salaried office you would be required to leave practice.

The Judicial Office runs a work-shadowing scheme which allows lawyers to shadow a judge both in and out of court for up to three days to learn more about what is involved. Applicants can choose to shadow a circuit judge in the criminal and civil courts, a district judge in the civil or criminal courts or a tribunal judge. Time spent on the scheme counts for up to 12 CPD hours. Information on the scheme can be found at **www.judiciary.gov.uk** or by emailing workshadowing@judiciary.gsi.gov.uk.

The Judicial Office website also carries information on judicial roles, including a number of 'day in the life' profiles written by serving judges. If your own practice background has not involved much court work, it would be well worth spending an afternoon sitting in a court room to get a sense of the court process and the role of the judge.

The application process comprises the completion of an application form including a self-assessment against specified qualities and abilities, the nomination of judicial and professional references and assurances as to good character. Applications are sifted and candidates meeting the requirements are asked to sit a qualifying test. Most tests are now conducted online and are likely to comprise a set of multiple choice questions. Frequently candidates are advised in advance to look at particular pieces of legislation and/or procedure rules and are required to apply that information against a case presented in the test. The test is designed to test your suitability to becoming a judge and is used to decide which candidates will be invited to attend a selection day. At least twice as many applicants than posts to be filled are interviewed. They usually also undertake a role-playing exercise in which they will assume the role of the judge while actors will perform the roles of parties appearing before the court or tribunal or fellow members of a tribunal.

Throughout the selection process applicants are assessed against specified qualities and abilities. You need to be able to demonstrate evidence that you meet these criteria by citing specific examples from your professional career as a solicitor or in another capacity such as experience as a school governor or involvement in a community group or charity. At the interview you will again be asked, for example, 'Give me an example of when you worked as part of a team'. The JAC's qualities and abilities are set out below. The important thing is to bear them in mind and periodically jot down examples which you can use when it comes to applying. There is often only a three week window between the launch of a recruitment exercise and the deadline for applications to be submitted. You will not have time with the day job to search your memory. The clear message if you want to apply to become a judge is plan ahead and start planning early.

1. Intellectual capacity:

    • High level of expertise in your chosen area or profession.
    • Ability to absorb and analyse information quickly.
    • Appropriate knowledge of the law and its underlying principles, or the ability to acquire this knowledge where necessary.

2. Personal qualities:

    • Integrity and independence of mind.
    • Sound judgment.
    • Decisiveness.
    • Objectivity.
    • Ability and willingness to learn and develop professionally.
    • Ability to work constructively with others.

3. An ability to understand and deal fairly:

    • An awareness of the diversity of the communities which the courts and tribunals serve and an understanding of differing needs.
    • Commitment to justice, independence, public service and fair treatment.
    • Willingness to listen with patience and courtesy.

4. Authority and communication skills:

- Ability to explain the procedure and any decisions reached clearly and succinctly to all those involved.
- Ability to inspire respect and confidence.
- Ability to maintain authority when challenged.

5. Efficiency:

- Ability to work at speed and under pressure.
- Ability to organise time effectively and produce clear reasoned judgments expeditiously (including leadership and managerial skills where appropriate).

Part C: Teaching law – Leslie Moran

Legal education opens up a range of career pathways for a solicitor. Drawing on my own experience and knowledge of higher education, I will in this section:

- give a brief sketch of the sector and some of the careers within it;
- identify some of the factors you need to consider if you are thinking about a career 'teaching law';
- explore some of the pros and cons of a career in education; and
- give some guidance on how best to develop a career in legal education.

Teaching law or a career in legal education?

The phrase 'teaching law' really doesn't do justice to the wide range of careers and activities open to you as a qualified solicitor working in legal education. There are many different types of educational jobs. They are in a wide range of educational institutions: schools, colleges of further education and universities. Many of these jobs are in the public sector but there are increasing numbers of legal education providers in the private sector. Be aware that:

- different types of educational institution may offer a different career pathway;
- the criteria for entry may be significantly different;
- the career expectations and rewards may vary considerably; and
- the work can differ dramatically.

In a secondary school you will spend a lot of time in the classroom. At the other end of the spectrum, in a research-led university, research, not teaching, may be your primary focus. Solitary library-based legal research and writing and management, rather than face-to-face contact with students, may be the norm. In other university posts the focus is much more on

83

teaching, both face-to-face and distance learning. And there are many variations in between.

Legal education work: teaching, research, management

Work in the legal education sector is made up of three basic components.

1. Teaching

The type of teaching you do, the topics you teach and the students you work with may differ dramatically. Learning and teaching strategies may vary depending upon the level of course and the type of student you are working with. Teaching law in a secondary school may involve teaching a wide range of legal topics under the umbrella of an 'A' level course in law. There may also be opportunities to teach across a range of related subjects, e.g. politics, citizenship education and general studies. Teaching on one of the many pre or post-degree legal practice courses, the focus of learning and teaching will be legal procedure and relevant skills for day-to-day work in a lawyer's office. Teaching in a higher education institution is likely to be a very different experience, for in this context you have more autonomy over curriculum content. For example, my current undergraduate company law course touches on the metaphysics of corporate personality, policy debates about gender diversity on boards of public companies, comparative corporate governance as well as the more traditional topics such as the statute and case law on directors' duties or lifting the veil of incorporation. Some might describe it as 'ivory tower' but I think of it as a project that develops critical and analytical skills, emphasises communication skills and research skills and builds a knowledge base that provides the social, political and cultural context central to an understanding of law and legal practice. The only restraints on curriculum design in this context apply to the core subjects and options often reflect personal interests of individual lecturers.

2. Research

Research on law is primarily undertaken in universities. Some universities give this a greater priority than others. Changes to university funding are likely to lead to research being undertaken in a smaller number of universities. Legal research you undertake while working as a solicitor may give you the skills necessary for research in a university. But legal research is much wider than library-based studies of cases and legislation. Research in law is incredibly diverse in topic and method. It ranges from doctrinal analysis and empirical sociological studies of law to critical scholarship and research that draws upon the humanities, such as literary studies of legal texts. Universities also provide opportunities for multi and inter-disciplinary legal research. Working with architects, theatre, film and television scholars and psychologists are just some of the more recent areas of legal scholarly collaboration.

3. Management and administration

Management and administration is an inevitable part of the job in legal education. The type and volume you do will vary from institution to institution and depend on whether you are in a permanent post or working on a freelance basis. In traditional universities, management has always been by academics while in other institutions this is less often the case. It may also be a factor in your career planning. Solicitors working in education are well represented in the higher management positions of many educational institutions. For some administration is an intrusive chore. For others it offers a rewarding career pathway within education.

Pros and cons

Because of the many different legal educational careers open to you it is difficult to generalise about pros and cons. Let me begin with a few 'pros':

- Inspiring and facilitating learning can be hugely rewarding.
- Positions in higher education still provide many opportunities to develop a passion for law, be it in developing existing or new courses or in undertaking legal research.
- The combination of teaching, research and management provides a variety of interactions and potentially a range of career pathways in legal education more generally.
- You potentially have a far greater degree of control over how and where you work. It's not necessarily a job where you are in the office '9 to 5' or '8 to 7' and while 'long holidays' is more myth than reality, term times are different from student vacation periods. Working from home to prepare classes or doing your research may be an option.
- Many of the jobs will come with public sector pension provision.
- There may be more opportunities for flexible working and easier integration of caring responsibilities.

Some of the 'cons' are the following:

- The financial rewards may be more limited (at least compared to the remunerative areas of private practice).
- Juggling the three different roles can be difficult, often resulting in long hours and no clear work boundaries.
- Mixed abilities of students can be very challenging.

- In many institutions there has been an increase in bureaucratic and managerial demands.

Career planning

If you are thinking of moving into education you need to engage in some careful planning. There are opportunities but you are not necessarily pushing at an open door if you plan to take your career in an educational direction. Having studied law and worked in law doesn't necessarily mean that you automatically satisfy the needs of legal educators. The following is a check list of activities and things to consider:

1. Review your career to date and identify the skills and knowledge set that is relevant to working in education.
2. Identify the type and balance of work you prefer and aspire to: teaching, research, management and administration.
3. Identify the type of educational institution you wish to work in and the type of student you want to work with.
4. Research the relevant qualification expectations and identify your qualification strengths and gaps.

    (a) Is a teaching qualification necessary? If you plan to teach in schools it is likely to be a prerequisite. If you are planning a career in a university it may be something you undertake during your probationary period.
    (b) Is a postgraduate law qualification essential? For example, universities increasingly expect law academics to have completed at least a postgraduate academic qualification if not a PhD prior to appointment.

5. Maximise networking opportunities. Opportunities to do this include the following:

    (a) Undertaking a postgraduate degree.
    (b) Attending academic conferences, seminars, workshops.
    (c) Building links with local education providers.

6. Some previous teaching experience will serve you well. Part-time teaching provides an opportunity for you to get some experience and make links with an educational institution that offers legal studies.
7. If you are interested in research, think about writing articles for journals. Writing book reviews and case commentaries is a good place to start.

Some final thoughts

Legal education continues to provide career opportunities. Law has become one of the most popular choices for undergraduate study. While changes to the funding of higher education have had an impact on all subjects, the early signs are that legal education has not been unduly affected by the changes. A return to the possibility of entering the profession without a degree may in due course cause a decline in university legal education, but its impact is likely to be uneven. If the rewards to be gained by moving into legal education are not necessarily financial, there are many others. While the division between legal education and the world of legal practice has been growing, these two worlds are not necessarily sealed off from each other. There is potential for dialogue. Opportunities to cross the divide exist. All in all, there are many positive reasons for making a career change by moving into legal education and many career options within legal education.

Chapter 8

Working in-house

Kat Gibson

In 2008, approximately a quarter (23 per cent) of solicitors holding practising certificates worked in the employed sector. This sector includes those solicitors working for local government or the Armed Forces, the Government Legal Service, not-for-profit or charity organisations, the Criminal Prosecution Service and those working for companies, in commerce and industry. The latter group comprises around 15,000 solicitors (or in-house counsel). The first part of this chapter will focus on commerce and industry, but the principles also apply to working in other organisations.

The role of the in-house lawyer

Within commerce and industry, the role of in-house solicitors varies greatly, as does the department or function in which they work. Most undertake legal case or advice work themselves, but the amount of this will depend. Some in-house counsel take on an oversight or strategic role, managing external law firms or coordinating advice. Others have a more 'hands on' approach as more generalist lawyers, taking on anything that comes across their desk. Around half work in departments with three or less legal staff and a quarter work on their own. Almost all take on administrative work along with legal work.

Despite the differences in work, function and structure, in-house counsel all advise their employer on how the law applies to their business. They identify risk and look for ways to mitigate it. Their role is to seek to ensure compliance for the company, looking for practical solutions to any problems or innovative ways to achieve outcomes. This has been described as being both 'a business person who happens to be a lawyer' and 'the conscience of the business'. Both quotes go some way to describing the role of in-house counsel, but the reality is somewhere in between.

Career paths

It is unusual for solicitors to begin their career in-house. Indeed, most legal counsel trained in private practice, with only seven per cent training in-house. While it is possible to train in-house, most solicitors train, qualify and gain experience in private practice before moving into an in-house team. This is primarily due to the fact that most in-house departments are under-resourced. This means that they do not have the time or resource to devote to training and that all new hires need to hit the ground running and take on a large amount of responsibility and autonomy very quickly.

Most of those moving in-house do so in the early part of their career, between two and five years' post-qualification experience (PQE). There is no 'right time' to move, however those moving before having two years' experience could struggle due to the autonomy and responsibility mentioned above and those moving later in their careers may find it hard to adapt to the different focus of the advice.

Those who choose to move in-house have a number of reasons for doing so. Often cited is the wish to escape from targets, time recording and billing. While it is true that most in-house departments don't have these, there are other pressures on the in-house counsel. The loss of the billable hour means that in-house functions need to find other ways to measure their performance and value. This usually means that the team will have specific objectives and competency requirements, assessed in appraisals and other metrics to hit (such as measuring time saved, fees avoided or keeping track of external counsel fees).

Working in-house

Working in-house is different from working in private practice. The primary difference is the ethos and function of the legal department. The legal department's focus is on both legal compliance and enabling business, with the lawyer acting as a business partner. While it is correct that the best commercial firms also apply this principle, the private practice law firm does not usually take this approach to advice. This approach includes looking both at the law and the risk landscape as well as the commercial factors and the 'bigger picture' to ensure that the recommendations given are the best fit both legally and commercially. This requires the in-house counsel to know their business and their clients, to understand the commercial strategy of the organisation and the key drivers for the proposals.

In addition, it is important for the lawyer to realise that his or her role is not to constantly advise the business people that the law prevents them from doing what they wish to do. This leads to the team being referred to as the 'no department' or the 'business blockers'. Instead, when a potential legal problem arises, counsel should advise the business people of the legal problem and work with them to reach their goals without legal risk. This problem solving, solutions-focussed attitude is crucial to ensure that the business is able to achieve its aims, without breaching regulations or accruing significant legal risk.

To greater align the legal team to the business, the legal team's objectives are usually associated with the company's. In this way, the aims of the lawyer are closely connected to those of their clients. The company's annual business plan and long range plan will be supported by the plans of the legal department. Similarly, the workloads of the in-house team will be prioritised to match those of the business. This ensures that the legal team is working on the issues which matter most to the business or can better assist its commercial enterprise. This does not mean that compliance or routine legal tasks are neglected, but it does mean that the business's lawyers are spending the majority of their time where they can add the most value. This means that the lawyers' understanding of the business and their ability to see both legal and commercial risks can be put to the best use; with external counsel picking up the overspill.

In a law firm, it is usual to be working on a few long-term projects at a time. However, in-house, there are more quick-answer type of problems and questions to deal with simultaneously. These change on a daily basis, as new ideas and work flows are developed by the business. How to manage this constantly changing workload, as well as deciding what is most important, is something which in-house counsel need to acclimatise themselves to – especially given that this will change several times throughout the day.

Key skills

In-house lawyers need to think more quickly on their feet, get to the core of each problem and find fast solutions. The in-house lawyer does not have sufficient time to reflect on, analyse or research an issue. Clients do not want to discuss legal issues or need an academic, lengthy, piece of written advice. They need quick and pragmatic advice that they can understand. The tone of the advice is important, as well as keeping it concise, relevant and clear. All advice must be delivered in plain English, in 'business speak' and should be tailored to the audience. Where there are legal uncertainties concerning an issue, clients need to be advised of this, along with the risks, a cost/benefit analysis and what their options are. The client is the decision-maker, but the lawyer should consider both the business and legal problems and make a recommendation.

Key differences between working in private practice and in-house

The in-house department itself is very different to a law firm. The business of a law firm is law. The sole focus of a law firm is producing legal work. Therefore, the lawyers are the core of the organisation and everyone else exists to support them to deliver the finished product. The success of a lawyer is evaluated on the quality of his or her work, and, at senior levels, possibly the ability to generate business. In contrast, the business of the company in which in-house solicitors work is not law. It will be something quite different, whether making a product or providing a different kind of service. While in-house counsel must still provide the highest quality work, solicitors are present in a company to support the business people to deliver their product or service.

As in-house counsel do not sell or manufacture the business's product or service, they are not seen as actually making money for the business. The legal team is usually considered to be a 'support function'. This means that the department needs to justify its existence, as the value and expense of legal advice is always under review. This includes the actual financial cost (whether external or internal) of advice as well as the quantity/quality of the added value. As a result, the benefits of using in-house counsel need to be clear. This is especially important when the benefits are non-tangible and non-financial. The legal team therefore does need to take a sales role, selling itself to its internal clients. This involves advertising the team's successes and is essentially the business development you would expect at a law firm, including newsletters and training. Also as a support function, the level of investment by the business in the legal team is limited – meaning that lawyers will have limited research tools, administrative support and equipment to carry out their role. For example, online resources are usually limited to one webtool, there are no secretaries or professional support lawyers (certainly no dictation), no (or basic) matter management software and perhaps not even a smartphone.

As an employee of a company, however, the in-house counsel will be subject to the same policies and entitlements as the other employees. This means that lawyers are more likely to be working flexibly or remotely. Most companies offer schemes to all employees that make it easier to balance work and home life. In addition, most companies offer attractive benefits packages (including enhanced maternity leave, private healthcare/dental and company cars) which are available to lawyers and non-lawyers alike. This also applies to salaries and bonuses; lawyers fit into pay grades and scales – along with all other employees. This can work to the lawyer's advantage, but usually it means that in-house counsel are paid less than their private practice peers.

In-house lawyers are integrated into the business itself. This means that they work alongside their internal clients, both literally and figuratively. Most in-house counsel work with their clients in office parks or buildings which are usually not city centre locations but are more likely to be on the outskirts, accessible from airports or roadways. In addition, in-house counsel will spend time visiting their clients 'on the job' – in factories, distribution centres, shops, restaurants, pubs, etc. – in order to gain a greater understanding of the business itself.

Relationship management

Relationships are equally as important to in-house counsel as to the private practice lawyer. All lawyers need to establish trust with their clients and to communicate with them effectively. In-house lawyers, just like private practice lawyers, need to take the time to network and meet their clients in order to understand their drivers and challenges. Attending company social events and conferences, as well meeting clients 'on the job' as above, are important ways of achieving this. It is also important for in-house counsel to seek feedback from their clients and to act on it. This allows in-house lawyers to understand how to improve and to ensure that they are providing the business with the support that they are looking for.

Being integrated into the business does not mean becoming a 'yes man' or losing your integrity. In-house counsel must be able to 'speak truth to power' and to deliver unpopular advice. Although in-house counsel must be close to their clients, find solutions to issues and attempt to facilitate the business's objectives, this should not be done at the mercy of the professional standards required of a solicitor. Instead, the solicitor must communicate this difficult message in the best way and must use his or her skills to influence and persuade the business towards a more compliant approach.

Business acumen and knowledge

Managing these difficult discussions is a skill that must be learnt by in-house lawyers as they develop their career. They must also learn and develop their business acumen and their understanding of both the company in which they work and the wider sector. They need to understand the outside influences on their business along with the internal issues. This in turn will develop their ability to find practical, workable solutions to legal issues and to make clear recommendations to the business, based on a balancing of commercial and legal factors. They should also develop their management skills, including people and project management. Senior lawyers within a legal department often have management responsibility for junior members, which is a greater role than simply supervising their legal work. The company will have a management structure and the in-house lawyer will be working within this as well as developing his or her own legal skills. The ability to influence peers and work effectively in a team is also important, as the legal department is a collaborative team, often with shared goals.

There is more emphasis on skills development in-house. Companies usually have formal structures and schemes in place for personal development, as well as more of a focus on the acquisition of the soft skills described above. This emphasis on development extends into career progression and succession planning, which again is usually managed within the company's overall programme. Law firms provide clear and defined career paths. You either become a partner or counsel, or you gain good experience and then leave. The end goal is clear and how to get there usually is as well. However, in the in-house world, the career path is more varied and not as defined. For this reason, it is more important to have defined career goals and it is here where the company's career development programme is important.

Career development and diversification

That said, the ability to progress through promotion is limited in-house, as the hierarchies are strictly observed but flatter. This could mean that the head of legal (vice president or executive grade) has a team of lawyers reporting directly to him or her. Progression is an issue even in teams where there are longer reporting lines, as there are fewer positions, meaning that lawyers stay in role for longer periods or do not have any obvious roles available as logical 'next steps'. This means that most progression opportunities are in the broadening of roles and the taking on of new responsibilities, rather than promotions. Lawyers will be developed to expand their legal expertise into new areas or develop their management capabilities, for example. In fact, there is always the ability to move to other departments within the organisation, such as public affairs, marketing, HR, finance or sales (for example). In-house counsel often diversify their roles, given that they have become so close to the business.

This diversification is an important element of working in-house. While specialist in-house roles do exist, most in-house roles involve the lawyer broadening his or her expertise and taking on different types of work. This broadening also means that advice becomes more commercial and less strictly legal. In-house lawyers should be prepared to take on anything that the business requires, meaning that they may eventually move away from being a specialist to being a generalist. This is certainly true of most general counsel, who will have done as much as possible in order to understand the business, appreciate risk and how to manage it.

Pros and cons

Working in-house is not for everyone. However, those that do decide to make the move often never return to private practice. As well as receiving the early autonomy and responsibility mentioned above, legal counsel are involved in key business decisions and can be valued strategic business partners. The in-house lawyer will be advising on more than the law and is more likely to be involved in a project from the outset through to completion. The advice and the approach are more practical and more strategic and therefore the lawyer has more of a role to play in the development of the organisation's aims and objectives. This, in turn, allows the lawyer to hone his or her non-legal skills and to become more adept in learning new areas of law. The flat hierarchy means that most in-house counsel are exposed to high quality, interesting work at all stages of their careers. There is the chance to develop new skills and even to decide to progress as a manager or move away from law. In some companies, there may even be the possibility to move between jurisdictions and to do some international work. Working for a commercial enterprise means that in-house counsel will benefit from their employer's reward packages (including enhanced benefits) and flexibility in ways of working. In-house lawyers are usually more informed buyers of legal services, having knowledge of the law firm with its business development and billing targets.

Some do find that working in-house is not for them. They find that those elements of the role highlighted above do not work for them and that they would prefer to return to private practice or look at other alternatives. The lack of support and supervision can be off-putting for some lawyers, as well as the need to take on a new type of role, such as project management. Black letter law and academic discussion of the same is less important in-house as the focus is on practical solutions. Becoming a cost for the business can also take its toll; being far less resourced and needing to justify your existence can be difficult. In addition, the metrics required to show the value added or to measure success are challenging to create. In-house lawyers still need to develop their relationships with clients and therefore business development is still required. A particular issue is the need to generalise and diversify. This can result in the loss of a specialism which a lawyer may have cultivated for his or her whole career. The lack of career progression and opportunities for advancement can be frustrating and can mean that lawyers spend far longer at a certain grade than perhaps they would in private practice. Moving into commerce and industry is also not likely to mean that the hours of work and stress levels are any less; it is unusual to find a 'nine to five' legal role. The salaries in-house are not commensurate with private practice, due to the internal grading and benchmarking exercises.

Conclusion

In order to be a successful in-house lawyer, it is important to be a good lawyer and have an excellent understanding of the law. An in-house lawyer, while a business person, is a solicitor first and foremost. Training in private practice is a good way to gain this, whether through training at a law firm or through a secondment from an in-house traineeship. This is due to the supervision provided in a law firm environment, as well as having a greater variety of clients, which allows the lawyer to develop confidence and experience in dealing with both a variety of legal issues and a variety of personalities. In addition, an understanding of the law firm and how it works will be extremely useful to in-house lawyers as consumers of legal services. It also reinforces the professional standards, ethics and integrity required of a solicitor – regardless of practice type.

Having a good grounding in law is important, as having an in-house role means that the lawyer must be confident in the law and how to apply it. This understanding is critical in being able to give practical options and solutions to the internal client, as well as making clear recommendations. In-house lawyers do not give advice and sit on the fence, but must advise the business which route to take and why. These recommendations require skills of persuasion, as the most legally compliant option may not be the best commercially. Counsel must navigate between the two and then sell the solution to the business.

These skills are what set in-house lawyers apart from private practice lawyers. As well as practically applying law and influencing management, in-house lawyers must be able to communicate effectively, possess financial and business acumen and understand their business and their sector. They must also be able to identify non-legal risk, as sometimes these can be more important and more difficult than the legal elements. In-house lawyers need to build rapport with their clients and become trusted advisors. They should be seen as business enablers and strategic business partners. This alignment to the business is key to success.

In-house lawyers need to have a 'can do' attitude. They should have the desire to learn and develop in new areas of law, as well as to get their hands dirty – by taking ownership issues and for problem solving. They should demonstrate real leadership and think about where they can add the most value. They should broaden their role, taking on new responsibilities and finding new and innovative ways to support the business and deliver advice. That said, it is important to prioritise and ensure that the work done is aligned to the business's strategic objectives, with all other work out-sourced or automated.

While in-house lawyers need a different skill set from their private practice cousins, the similarities are clear. Both need to be good lawyers with a strong underpinning of professional ethics. There is an increasing amount of blurring between the lines as law firms begin to adopt different ways of working and there is a certain amount of overlap between in-house departments and law firms. In any event, in-house lawyers will always be consumers of legal services and will continue to work alongside the traditional practice model.

Working in-house is an attractive option for those who want to take on a challenging role that is constantly changing and developing. Involvement in the commercial strategy of the business, along with the added responsibility, is an excellent and exciting opportunity. The specific skills required are an asset to any lawyer, regardless of practice type. However, the lack of promotional opportunities and the walk away from specialisms should be seriously considered by anyone considering an in-house role. Provided that the lawyer is aware of this, then the in-house sector presents an interesting and rewarding career path to follow.

CASE STUDY: Private practice to local government

Tell us a little about yourself (where you practise, what type of firm, what work you currently undertake)

I currently work in local government (a small district authority in a rural area). The legal team is very small. While to date I have concentrated on mainly planning matters (s.106 agreements, advice on planning law and enforcement notices) and licensing work, I have also been heavily involved in a large commercial property transaction (managing external lawyers) and liaising with officers for the negotiations and sensitive high profile litigation (working closely with counsel). This work has been outside of my specialism.

What specialism/practice area did you initially gain?

Environmental law (first as a research fellow for a charity then working as a paralegal for large commercial firms in private practice).

What specialism/practice area did you develop?

Planning and the law around compulsory purchase orders (CPOs).

How did you achieve this?

I developed my planning specialism through studying part-time for a Diploma in Planning Law and Practice while working as a paralegal in a regional commercial law firm and then qualifying into a planning and environmental law team in the same firm. I developed my CPO specialism through working on a retail-led redevelopment scheme while in private practice. I developed this specialism in my move to local government (I moved to a large unitary authority in the north to work on the housing renewal programme). Since joining a small rural authority I have undertaken mainly planning and licensing work and some environmental (contaminated land and Part II of the Environmental Protection Act 1990). But I have also been involved in a few big projects as mentioned already. I am currently learning about the procurement regime to support officers.

How long did it take?

Three to six years (to develop the planning and CPO specialism).

What did you find positive about the experience?

It broadened my experience and made me more employable. Joining local government has been another change and a big cultural shock. I have yet to tell whether it is a positive step in my career!

Local government is very political. It is a very challenging environment to navigate. I have had to cross over and get involved in areas of law not within my specialism (for example property, litigation, licensing and most recently procurement). This is challenging but interesting (providing there is the support/training resource).

What was not so positive?

In becoming a planning lawyer I have not enjoyed having to deal with a large number of s.106 agreements and highway agreements. In moving to local government it has taken me some time to adapt to the very different culture of local government.

What is the one thing that you wished you had known before changing or, indeed, before specialising?

That I would end up doing so many s.106 agreements. That I would find the culture of local government so different to private practice. My work/life balance has greatly improved since moving away from private practice and I appreciate the more flexible work environment. However I have struggled to adapt to a workplace where the resources are poor and performance management tends to be, in my experience, weak.

What was the most difficult thing about changing your specialism/practice area?

The culture of local government.

What tips would you give anyone else thinking of changing their specialism/practice area?

I think it is exciting and interesting to broaden your experience and undertake work outside of your specialism. I think doing so makes you more resilient in times of recession and the job more interesting. However there is the danger of dabbling and being negligent. So you have to have the proper resources/supervision/training in place to help make the change.

Going into local government from private practice is a big cultural change. Local government is going through a lot of change in response to funding cuts from central government and the passing of legislation such as the Localism Act 2011. This is impacting on the workplace and traditional ways of working/delivering services are being challenged.

I would recommend anyone thinking of making this move to thoroughly research the set up/team they will be working with first before making any decision. Ideally you want to know the reputation of the people and respect them as lawyers. You want to find out the relationship between legal services and the rest of the council. Are legal services held in high regard? Or are legal services marginalised? What is the client/officer relationship like? What is the relationship like between officers and councillors? You need to think whether you want to work for a large authority or a small one. If working for a small authority, you have to be prepared to get involved with work outside of your specialism. I think there is more opportunity to get involved with a greater diversity of work and to make a bigger impact in a smaller authority than a larger one.

Chapter 9

International opportunities

Julia Bateman

Setting the scene

When speaking about an international legal career we can conjure up images of anything from a glamorous office in an exotic location, to multi-lingual diplomatic negotiations, to aid-related work in a developing country. However these scenarios only go some way in encapsulating the breadth of the work that might fall within the sphere of 'international'. This chapter seeks to:

- highlight the different opportunities available and type of work that can lend an international element to practice;
- give advice on formal routes to working and qualifying abroad where they exist.

The world is changing. The global economy has shifted and progress is being driven by emerging markets. Technology and regulatory changes have also brought about further developments and innovations. In 2013, the global legal services market is forecast to have a value of £450.5 billion, an increase of 23.3 per cent since 2008.

Such changes lead to dynamic career opportunities both at the early stages of qualification and in terms of the developing areas of law and practice. International career opportunities can range from a short-term internship, a seat as part of a training contract, a three-year posting or, ultimately, in a more senior role as a managing partner of an overseas office for a global law firm. An in-house role in a multi-national corporation can offer a significant cross-jurisdictional career. The Government Legal Service includes posts within the Foreign and Commonwealth Office.

Outside of traditional legal practice, lawyers and legal skills are in demand in international organisations. Legal teams play a key role in international organisations and the EU institutions in particular have a sizeable legal service. Those with a legal background also play a key role in jobs relating to developing legislation and policy. A qualified legal professional is in a strong position to demonstrate the intellectual, analytical and communication qualities as transferable skills between disciplines.

International legal work can require so much more than the law itself. Language skills are of course important. Those who have studied law with a foreign language are in a strong position to set out their motivation and interest in an international career as well as the linguistic skill itself. That said it is never too late to learn a language and the rise of internet-based learning and learning on the move through podcasts, for example, do not mean time-consuming classroom-based learning. Do not however over-state your language skills in relation to a foreign language on an application lest the interviewer happens to switch fluently into that language!

Working with a client seeking to enter new markets will involve working with lawyers and business in one or more jurisdictions. Diplomatic skills and the ability to operate in new and diverse cultural environments are critical and should not be underestimated. Networking skills and commu-nications skills are key. Much of the work supporting a client will be additional to black letter law advice, for example advising on the local regulatory and business environment; dealing with government relations; due diligence; and regulatory compliance.

Close to home

As a starting point though it is worth remembering that you don't neces-sarily have to look to working overseas to have an international element to your work. Advising clients with an international reach who operate in a number of jurisdictions is increasingly the norm in large law firms in the UK.

Indeed the role of London as a global legal hub and the leading position of the UK law firms on the global stage can lend an international flavour to a UK-based seat. With centuries of experience to draw on, it is the world leader in international finance and business services.

England and Wales is predominantly the jurisdiction of choice for inter-national dispute resolution. More international and commercial arbitra-tions take place in London than in any other city in the world.

Parties are likely to find experts in the subject matter of the dispute, however complex or technical it may be. Ninety per cent of commercial cases handled by London law firms now involve an international party.

English law is predominantly the law of choice for global commerce. Legal careers that are international by virtue of their location may actually be based on advising a foreign client in an overseas jurisdiction (often an emerging market) on a transaction based on English law.

Each law firm operates its own regimes relating to training contract seats and newly qualified positions. Those looking for an international element to a seat during a training contract or as a newly qualified solicitor should seek advice within your law firm as to the type of work and client base in the dispute resolution teams and sector specific.

Moreover as certain business and industrial sectors grow, and where the UK has strengths, such as in the energy, mining and minerals and creative industries, those areas of work increasingly offer international opportunities. Indeed, a significant amount of international interaction arises in instances where law firms are advising international client companies about setting up in England and Wales. This ranges from advising on rules around setting up a company in the UK and local licensing provisions, to immigration requirements, social security and employment law.

A European perspective

The European Union offers a multitude of opportunities for international experience. Those international law firms with offices throughout Europe often offer secondments as part of a training contract or postings for qualified solicitors. Firms that have an extensive business relationship or are part of a network can also offer exchanges and secondments in a less formal manner. The Law Society's Brussels office itself offers secondments to trainee solicitors.

EU law has opened up significant new areas of practice. Competition law and trade law are key areas of law with Brussels offices of UK and US law firms long since leading the way in this area. Core areas of law stemming from the internal market such as company law and financial services, public procurement and tax are big business areas as well as consumer law and environment. Not to mention newer areas of EU law such as criminal justice and private client matters.

Moreover there is a formal regime for EU citizens qualified as a lawyer in one member state to operate in another. The regime to regulate the cross-border supply of legal services and the rules designed to facilitate the establishment of a lawyer in a different member state other than his or her own has been in force for a number of years. There are three key pieces of legislation that affect the legal profession:

*   Lawyers' Services Directive 1977 (77/249/EEC).
*   Establishment of Lawyers Directive 1998 (98/5/EC).
*   Recognition of Professional Qualifications Directive 2005 (2005/36/EC).

In addition, the Directive on Services in the Internal Market (2006/123/EC) which regulates the provision of services in the European Union also touches on the legal profession.

The Law Society's International Division seeks to assist those wanting to become established in another EU member state with information and support during the process.

The Lawyers' Services Directive (temporary provision)

The Lawyers' Services Directive 1977 (77/249/EEC) governs the provision of services by an EU/EEA/Swiss lawyer in a member state other than the one in which he or she gained his or her title – known as the 'host state'. Its purpose is to facilitate the free movement of lawyers, but it does not deal with establishment or the recognition of qualifications.

The directive provides that a lawyer offering services in another member state – a 'migrant' lawyer – must do so under his or her home title. Migrating lawyers may undertake representational activities under the same conditions as local lawyers, save for any residency requirement or requirement to be a member of the host bar.

However, they may be required to work in conjunction with a lawyer who practises before the judicial authority in question. For other activities the rules of professional conduct of the home state apply without prejudice with respect for the rules of the host state, notably confidentiality, advertising, conflicts of interest, relations with other lawyers and activities incompatible with the profession of law.

Permanent establishment under home title

The Establishment Directive entitles lawyers who are qualified in, and are citizens of, a member state to practise on a permanent basis under their home title in another EU/EEA member state or Switzerland. The practice of law permitted under the Directive includes not only lawyers' home state law, community law and international law, but also the law of the member state in which they are practising – the 'host' state.

However, this entitlement requires that a lawyer wishing to practise on a permanent basis registers with the relevant bar or Law Society in that state and is subject to the same rules regarding discipline, insurance and professional conduct as domestic lawyers. Once registered, the European lawyer can apply to be admitted to the host state profession after three years without being required to pass the usual exams, provided that he or she can present evidence of effective and regular practice of the host state law over that period.

Re-qualification as a full member of the host state legal profession

Re-qualification is governed by the new Recognition of Professional Qualifications Directive 2005 (2005/36/EC), which replaced the Diplomas Directive 1989 (89/48/EEC). Article 10 of the Establishment of Lawyers Directive 1998 (98/5/EC) is basically an exemption from the regime foreseen by the

Recognition of Professional Qualifications Directive. (Note: this Directive is currently under review.)

The basic rules are that a lawyer seeking to re-qualify in another EU/EEA member state or Switzerland must show that he or she has the professional qualifications required for the taking up or pursuit of the profession of lawyer in one member state and is in good standing with his or her home bar.

The member state where the lawyer is seeking to re-qualify may require the lawyer to either complete an adaptation period (a period of supervised practice) not exceeding three years, or take an aptitude test to assess the ability of the applicant to practise as a lawyer of the host member state. The test only covers the essential knowledge needed to exercise the profession in the host member state and it must take account of the fact that the applicant is a qualified professional in the member state of origin.

Traineeship in the EU institutions

A good way to experience the EU institutions is to actually work within them. Paid traineeships of five months with the European Commission (or some executive bodies and agencies of the European institutions like, for instance, the European External Action Service or Executive Agency for Competitiveness and Innovation) are offered twice a year. These start on either 1 March or 1 October each year. There is an open and transparent recruitment process and information can be found on the website (**www.europa.eu**). These traineeships offer a fascinating and rewarding insight into the workings of the EU institutions and brings to life the interactions more often studied on the pages of a textbook.

Up to 1300 places are offered each session spread amongst the 28 member states (and some placements for candidate countries). By undertaking such a placement you get hands-on experience in the international and multicultural environment that can be enriching for your future career. There are placements within the Legal Service itself or lawyers find themselves drawn to the legislative and policy directorates-general dealing with justice, internal market or competition.

A less formal way to gain EU experience can be through seeking opportunities within a Member of the European Parliament's office for a short-term period (**www.europarl.org.uk**) or in response to a recruitment advertisement. A legal background is a strong selling point for an office dealing with the development and enacting of legislation.

Doubling up

The effects of globalisation mean that the type of transactions carried out by international businesses demand multi-disciplinary and multi-jurisdictional legal advice. Therefore, in addition to seeking out opportunities to work in different jurisdictions on a case-specific or short or long-term basis some lawyers seeking an international legal career look to actually qualify in one or more jurisdictions in addition to the one where they first qualified. International firms with overseas networks and offices often look to recruit dual-qualified lawyers to bolster their existing expertise and international capacity both at home and abroad.

While the majority of jurisdictions will require lawyers from overseas to undertake the full law degree and qualification route of that country, a small number of jurisdictions do offer a conversion route.

For instance, England and Wales offers a route to qualification for overseas lawyers called the Qualified Lawyers Transfer Scheme (QLTS) (see **www.sra.org.uk/solicitors/qlts.page**). This allows overseas lawyers to undertake a series of assessments to convert their home qualification into that of a solicitor of England and Wales.

The QLTS does not make any distinction between lawyers who have their first qualification from a common law or a civil law jurisdiction and most foreign lawyers are eligible for direct access to the QLTS assessments. This means that no additional academic study is necessary, such as a common law-based law degree, before taking the QLTS test. However, some people do decide to take their QLTS exams while studying for an LLM postgraduate degree.

Transatlantic dialogue

Many English qualified lawyers seek out the USA for opportunities. The US legal system has its basis in the common law tradition of English law and there are over 1,100,000 licensed lawyers in the United States, making it the world's biggest legal profession.

As admittance to the legal profession varies from state to state, acceptance of applications by foreign lawyers or those with foreign law degrees to sit the state bar exam depend on the rules set by the relevant state regulator.

Some state bars may require the applicant to take further courses in US law at an ABA approved law school, or some may take into account time spent in practice in the home jurisdiction. Working in New York City and access to the New York bar are seen as particularly attractive. The State of New York has over 147,000 active lawyers – it is one of the largest legal professions in the United States.

Information on the New York bar exam can be found on the website of the New York State Board of Law Examiners (**www.nybarexam.org**). Those who are eligible have successfully completed a programme of study at a law school outside of the United States that is both 'durationally and substantively' equivalent to a programme of study at an approved law school in the United States, and if required, an additional programme of study at an approved law school in the United States.

The New York State bar examination is administered twice a year in February and July. The bar examination contains two sections, the New York section which is given first and the Multistate Bar Examination (MBE) which is given last. The New York section consists of five essay questions and 50 multiple choice questions prepared by the New York Board, and one Multistate Performance Test question, developed by the National Conference of Bar Examiners. The MBE section consists of 200 multiple choice questions.

As admittance to the legal profession varies from state to state, acceptance of applications by foreign lawyers or those with foreign law degrees to sit the state bar exam depends on the rules set by the relevant state regulator.

In addition, 27 states have an alternative route for foreign lawyers to practise via a Foreign Legal Consultant license. This permits foreign lawyers restricted legal practice within that state on the basis of their home country qualifications and experience. Licenses are available in Alaska, Arizona, California, Connecticut, the District of Columbia, Florida, Georgia, Hawaii, Idaho, Illinois, Indiana, Louisiana, Massachusetts, Michigan, Minnesota, Missouri, New Jersey, New Mexico, New York, North Carolina, Ohio, Oregon, Pennsylvania, South Carolina, Texas, Utah and Washington.

The exact requirements to apply for the license and the permissions granted under that license vary between states; solicitors should therefore confirm the rules with the relevant state regulatory body.

Similar rules relate to temporary foreign legal consultants, enquires should be made with the regulator in a particular state for the exact rules as they may differ from the model rule set down by the American Bar Association.

Further afield

A number of dispute resolution centres have developed overseas, a development which lends itself to short-term and long-term international career opportunities for solicitors. For example, the economic boom in the Gulf has led to Dubai becoming the main hub for international law firms operating in the United Arab Emirates. The Dubai International Financial Centre is unique in that it has a legislative system consistent with English Common law and thus English lawyers are required to service a significant international client base.

The rise of Asia as a geo-political and economic power lends opportunities for solicitors to operate overseas in those jurisdictions. Singapore, for example, is a dynamic dispute resolution centre home to a large number of solicitors qualified in England and Wales. A high number of solicitors are registered as practising in Hong Kong (China). South Korea has recently taken steps to liberalise its legal services market and the first UK law firm received its approval to open an office there in July 2012. The opening of the market will be staged over the next six years in line with the EU–Korea Free Trade Agreement.

The Law Society's International Division can support solicitors interested in finding out more about the regulatory environment and local rules in key jurisdictions.

Building networks

The Law Society has a membership section devoted to international practice. We have members from all over the world, all of whom are interested in acquiring international knowledge and developing their business and their skills in an international context.

The Law Society itself is actively engaged in international organisations such as the International Bar Association, the Union Internationale des Avocats and LawAsia. These organisations assist bar associations to build links with other bar associations around the world to discuss and debate issues facing the legal professions. These opportunities allow us to build contacts and relationships which come in useful when we seek information on regulatory reforms or need to assist a solicitor directly in a particular jurisdiction.

These organisations also have individual membership packages. Each organisation offers opportunities to understand, build and enhance an international legal career.

For those starting out on their career there are a number of ways to begin building your networks.

At the early stages of a legal career, the European Law Students' Association (ELSA) may be of interest. With 38,000 members, ELSA is the world's largest independent law students' association. ELSA provides opportunities for international exchange, diversified legal education and personal professional development for law students and young lawyers. Its members are law students and recent graduates who have an academic focus and have demonstrated commitment to international issues.

ELSA operates primarily through its local groups, which are located at nearly 300 law faculties in universities throughout 42 countries in Europe. For more information, visit **www.elsa.org**. The European Young Bar Association is another pan-European group that can offer access to a network of lawyers around Europe. For more information, see **www.eyba.org**.

The Law Society's Junior Lawyers Division itself has run international weekends and includes an international theme in its annual conference.

The Association Internationale des Jeunes Avocats (AIJA) is a key organisation for lawyers seeking international opportunities. The aims of the association, amongst others, are to:

- encourage meetings and to promote cooperation and mutual respect between young lawyers from all countries around the world;
- defend the interests of young lawyers and to study questions of relevance to them; and
- help establish groups of young lawyers in countries and regions where none now exist.

An annual conference is supplemented by practice-specific conferences throughout the year in different jurisdictions. There is a UK chapter of AIJA which is a good starting point to access this growing network. More information about AIJA can be found at **www.aija.org**.

The International Bar Association (IBA) is the world's leading organisation of international legal practitioners, bar associations and law societies. It has a membership of more than 50,000 individual lawyers and over 200 bar associations and law societies spanning all continents. Since 2004, the IBA sought to attract young lawyers to join the association and become active and engaged in its various committees, groups and initiatives. Therefore, the Young Lawyers' Committee was founded with a clear focus on young colleagues and their aims and interests. The Committee has recently started an International Internship Programme, an initiative launched to provide a platform to law students and recent law graduates to get in touch with global law firms to assist them to secure overseas internships. For more information, visit **www.ibanet.org/PPID/Constituent/Young_Lawyers_Committee/Default.aspx**.

Another significant international organisation is the Union Internationale des Avocats. The organisation brings together over 2,000 individual members and 200 bar, federation and association members from more than 110 countries. It offers seminars, training sessions and other events throughout the year in several countries, which are also accredited for continuing education purposes. A decision has recently been taken to set up an International Young Lawyers Section. For more information, see **www.uianet.org**.

The American Bar Association (ABA) is the world's largest membership organisation of lawyers. It admits US qualified lawyers as well as lawyers qualified in other jurisdictions into their International Section. The ABA has a Young Lawyers Division which is equally internationally minded.

Seeking support

The Law Society works on behalf of its members to reduce barriers facing UK solicitors entering and working in overseas markets, and establishes and maintains links with international counterparts. The international department provides practical support, training, information and advice to law firms and legal professionals working abroad, or exploring international opportunities. We seek to increase business opportunities for our members. We use our market intelligence, our contacts and our international reputation to run a variety of initiatives to help our members develop their international links and understanding of the international marketplace. Members stay updated via our monthly e-newsletter, International Update.

Our Brussels office monitors developments in EU law to ensure that they are compatible with the UK legal system, raises awareness of EU law and of opportunities in Europe amongst solicitors and offers trainee solicitors a unique opportunity to undertake a six-month secondment in the Brussels office. Members stay updated via our monthly e-newsletter, *Brussels Agenda*.

For more information, please contact international@lawsociety.org.uk or brussels@lawsociety.org.uk.

Conclusion

There are many routes and aspects to an international legal career, as set out above. It can encompass a number of scenarios from dual-qualification, to permanent establishment, to interaction with a foreign client. The thread that joins all these together is a dynamic and flexible approach and an open mind!

Chapter 10

Work/life balance: how to find it

Sue Lenkowski

How to progress professionally by maintaining useful and interesting extracurricular activities

This book has already discussed in numerous chapters the importance of networking – it is a pervasive aspect of a legal career. It is, however, pertinent to consider it again within the context of this chapter as it can potentially add to the long hours culture.

People buy legal services from people they like; most clients are ill equipped to make an informed judgment on the quality of an individual's ability to deliver legal advice. Networking and getting involved in extracurricular activities are vital to provide you with the ability to show your personality and win new business or maintain or leverage business from existing clients.

So how can you maintain useful and interesting networks/activities?

The first mistake some lawyers make, and one which I made when setting up my own business, is to focus networking around activities and groups which consisted of professionals similar to you. When I set up my business I attended events aimed at new start ups and HR professionals. The new start up events were full of people trying to sell me something (including lawyers) and, in a similar vein, none of the attendees had the funds to purchase my services. Of course it was useful to share ideas and concerns about the challenges of self-employment, something which was important at the time, but it wasn't helping me win business. I quickly recognised that I had to limit these activities and start to do other things.

I took a couple of board positions, one on a career academy (full of local business people), and a trustee role on a citizen's advice bureau as an HR advisor. These were (and still are) unremunerated but they allowed me to broaden my network and, just as importantly, give something back to my local community and young people. This illustrates an important point about what you choose to do – always do something that you enjoy as it's hard to get involved in something after a long day at work if you don't enjoy it. For me these activities fit with both the target market of my business and my passion for young people and access to justice. Whatever you choose to do make sure it is consistent with your brand and what you are trying to achieve.

There are so many activities that you could get involved in, but below are a small selection of possibilities:

- Boards and charitable trusts such as Citizens Advice, NHS primary care trust, charities which have an impact on your local community, school governing bodies and community groups.
- Chambers of commerce, Junior Chamber International (JCI) young professionals network.
- Junior Lawyers Division (JLD).
- Local interest groups which have a focus allied to the area you practise.
- Trade groups.
- Charitable activities, e.g. fundraising, right to read schemes and community regeneration schemes.

In addition to these physical activities, consider activities in the virtual world – join groups and discussion boards on LinkedIn and regularly provide an update on something topical and get involved in discussions. Why not start to write a regular blog, not necessarily based on legal topics, to show you are a person not just a lawyer. Choose a subject you are genuinely interested in and see how many new connections you can make.

Reality of working hours/expectations

When sitting down to write about work/life balance, my first thought was that I am unqualified to write it. My early professional career was characterised by working 14-hour days tied to a Blackberry, often going into the office at weekends and being ill every time I took a holiday. I never quite managed to relax and would find myself giving everyone a piece of me who wanted it but making little or no time for myself. At the time I convinced myself that I enjoyed it, the rewards were fantastic and I was highly valued by my employers.

This anecdote is typical of many people working in the law. Some manage to sustain it, some burn out and some do something about it. I would like to think that I did something about it by setting up my own consultancy and while I am slightly less affluent, my life is more fun and my health is much better. My solution to leave the world of PAYE and work for myself was a risky decision especially as I set up my business just after the financial meltdown of 2008. But it was the right thing for me to do and the emotional rewards have outweighed the reduction in income.

Many of you reading this book may not have this option although **Chapter 11** on alternative careers may be worth a second read if you feel that you need to address your work/life balance and don't believe you will be able to achieve it as a solicitor.

The reality of long hours in many law firms is well known and it would be disingenuous to suggest otherwise. When researching this chapter I reviewed a survey of associates undertaken by Legal Week in July 2012 which makes for a sobering read. The full article, 'Off balance – associate work/life balance remains as elusive than ever', by Rachel Rothwell can be found at **www.legalweek.com**.

The survey looked at hours of work for associates and of the 258 lawyers who responded to the survey, 37 per cent said they were working 40 to 50 hours – significantly more than the 35-hour week expected of the average UK employee, but not out of kilter with the demands of the profession and the salaries on offer.

A third of respondents were working 51 to 60 hours per week, and a significant minority (18 per cent) worked 61 to 70 hours in a week, which would amount to at least 10 hours a day if spread over six days. Worryingly, five per cent reported working up to 80-hour weeks – that would be nearly 11 hours' work per day if they worked every day of the week.

Only six per cent said they worked less than 40 hours.

So is it inevitable that a career in private practice will lead to long hours? The answer I believe is largely yes, certainly in the city, but how long you work can be managed and too many people make longer and longer hours the norm.

I used to work most Saturdays and Sundays and had done so for four years, probably in an attempt to replicate the behaviours of those around me. My manager left the firm and my new manager instructed me not to work at weekends. My objections and the angry reaction my new manager got to this request were quite extreme. I suggested that I would be unable to meet the needs of the business, I would miss deadlines and, in essence, I would be unable to do my job. My manager insisted I gave it a one-month trial.

Initially it was difficult, difficult because even within the first week I realised that by making Saturdays and Sundays the norm in my working week I would regularly look at something I needed to do and think 'I'll do that on Saturday/Sunday'. By no longer having these days to work it forced me to stop what I now know was a procrastination technique. It wasn't easy but I survived the trial and rarely after that time did I ever work at the weekend.

This may not work for you but if you are concerned about your work/life balance, take a long hard look at what you are doing with all the time you spend at work (or in your virtual office) and challenge whether you could do it differently.

Flexible part-time working

Gradually the legal sector is becoming more alive to flexible working and a number of firms have embraced the idea and are seeing considerable business benefits from retaining staff by changing their working patterns and practices.

To give you an idea of what has been done and what you may be able to achieve, consider the case studies below from the Law Society Diversity and Inclusion Charter (**www.lawsociety.org.uk/advice/diversity-inclusion-charter**).

Some names have been changed to preserve the anonymity of interviewees.

CASE STUDY: Job share

Context and background

Jane and Emma are both six years' PQE, and senior associates at Allen & Overy. The job share was instigated when Jane came back to work after having her second child and identified that she needed to find a different way of working. She identified Emma as a potential job share partner. Emma, at that time, was on maternity leave herself.

The initial agreement and contracting took some time in order to maximise the chances of the arrangement working effectively.

Practicalities

Both women work 8–10-hour days and also log on for 2–3 hours in the evening. They both work on Wednesday which provides valuable overlap and handover time. In respect of the billable work, the 'timer' is handed over at this point which ensures that the clients are not double billed. This is an area that they work hard to ensure they monitor. Handover involves a long email and a to-do list.

Where client demands require working late evenings and weekends, this is shared evenly. Both lawyers are willing to be flexible as the work requires meeting their clients' needs.

Productivity

Jane routinely achieves 35 per cent over her billable hours target. This is a 'supported arrangement' where 'trust is key', that is, knowing that the other person is responding and working just as you would in the same situation.

Flexibility is also a critical part of the success of this job share arrangement. The women highlighted the need to think of colleagues, the team and the fact that they are operating in a highly competitive market. Working on the same cases, they need to be seen as one person, so having a similar PQE and background is very helpful. This, in turn, enables them to delegate and focus on work requiring their experience and expertise.

CASE STUDY: Annualised hours

Context and background

Monica Burch is the senior partner at Addleshaw Goddard and chairs the firm's Governance Board. Qualifying in 1990, Monica worked for a US law firm in New York before returning to work as an associate at Theodore Goddard in 1999.

Monica did not start working flexibly until the birth of her third child in 2003. The decision to work part-time coincided with the arrival of her third child when she was already an equity partner.

Practicalities and challenges of working flexibly

> It was clear to me that the pattern of my practice required a five-day week, and I really thought about the workflow of a litigator. Although I need to work a five-day week and be available, I could manage my workflow to take a 10 per cent reduction in working time over each year.

The result is that Monica is able to take more time off to coincide with school holidays when courts are also closed. This effectively facilitates 10 weeks' holiday including half terms and August and provides important time with her family.

When Monica first suggested this solution she received a very positive response. On presenting the idea to the divisional managing partner, 'he didn't even suggest doing a trial period but agreed straight away.' Subsequently other partners have adopted this pattern of working and there are also other equity partners working four-day weeks.

> Working this way as senior partner, I can be fully involved in all the things I need to be involved in – throw myself into the role but have time with my family.
> ... working flexibly is easier to do as a partner – while you have clients to answer to, you don't have a partner to answer to. Being in command of your diary is important.
> Inevitably, as with any form of flexible working, there are plusses and minuses. In most commercial law firms which are client facing, you cannot partition off your time, you have to accept the high level of interruption. Being available and on call at weekends and holidays occurs at partner level for full-time workers and similarly in non-working time for those who carve out extra time.

Monica works closely with others who work flexibly and recognised early on that the key to success lies in understanding what patterns of flexibility suits her workflow and clients. This can vary according to practice area.

Monica identified the key advantages of her flexible working pattern as:

- Time off coincides with business workflow.
- Taking time off when clients and courts do, especially summer.
- It fulfils her senior partner role over a full week.
- She is fully available to clients.

Interruptions, especially during holidays, are viewed as an anticipated element of being a senior partner, in particular being available to deal with internal issues.

Having reached the top of her profession within a top 20 practice, Monica is fully supportive of different working patterns, 'I do think flexible working is possible.'

Shifting attitudes: flexible working is a business issue

The evidence of flexible work patterns becoming fully accepted at Addleshaw Goddard is the fact that Monica was elected to senior partner while working flexibly.

> Addleshaw Goddard accept the importance of retaining people – women (and younger men too) so flexible working is no longer outside the norm.

Monica acknowledged that flexible working still had the potential to be more career-limiting for men.

> We have male partners who work flexibly and I really don't think that working flexibly should be based on having children.

Monica Burch was clear that working flexibly was not purely for those with caring responsibilities.

> It is important to ensure that we retain our key talent, female and male.

CASE STUDY: Remote working

Context and background

Charlotte trained at Penningtons before qualifying as a solicitor specialising in company and commercial law in 2007. Charlotte now advises on corporate transactional work such as mergers and acquisitions, joint ventures and shareholder investments or company restructuring.

In August 2010, her husband (who was in the Armed Forces) was posted abroad to Gibraltar for two years. At four years' post-qualified, Charlotte faced difficult choices. Keen to continue her professional and career development, she started talking to her firm and the partners with whom she worked. Equally keen to keep Charlotte at Penningtons, they looked for and discussed various solutions.

Providing this solution enabled Penningtons to retain Charlotte's experience, knowledge and client relationships.

> My situation was unusual, the key to the solution is that it works for both sides, the solution emerged from lots of constructive conversations with partners about how we could make this work. If I had been a more junior lawyer, working in this way may not have been appropriate but this enabled me and the firm to keep my organisational knowledge and networks as well as my client relationships.

Practicalities and challenges of working flexibly and remotely

Working remotely posed few technical problems as the law firm was already operating across three offices.

This helped because the technology was already in place for senior management and business development people, with laptops and remote access software already set up.

> Now I work and can run transactions and delegate just as if I were in the office.

Most of her corporate transactional role is done remotely. Although unable to attend meetings, Charlotte stresses the importance of good communication.

> This arrangement is highly dependent on having good communication between me and the rest of the corporate team to ensure good workflow and efficient delivery. We used to have weekly teleconferencing between offices, now these are done via video conferencing so that I can join in.

Charlotte now has a zero hours contract which means that she works according to the workflow and for an hourly rate.

> I have worked until the early hours to meet transactional deadlines; the only difference is that it is at a distance.

Charlotte reports a very positive work/life balance as she can flex her life to fit her work schedule, ensuring that she responds quickly to any requests. From a firm's perspective, this arrangement provides highly efficient use of Charlotte as a key resource at critical times.

> Although this does ebb and flow as is normal in this area of practice, I was very busy in the run up to April with tax-based work but then August is always quiet.
>
> Workflow is good. Even if I am not in my office, I can keep an eye on work requests and can be very flexible. Working in this way has been a complete revelation – before I was working incredibly long hours as a typical transactional lawyer. This is still a big part of my life but no longer all of it. I had never imagined it was possible to combine really interesting work with the rest of my life. It can still be tough – as in this type of work the clients can be extremely demanding and I do work into the early hours to meet deadlines.

CASE STUDY: Tailored flexibility

Context and background

Robert was an associate solicitor working in commercial litigation when a flu-like virus triggered chronic fatigue syndrome (CFS), from which he has still not recovered. For more than a year he was bedridden, working entirely from home. However, for the last four years he has been able to work partly at home and partly in his employer's offices in the city.

His condition means that Robert suffers pain, tingling and other neurological symptoms and is obliged to use a wheelchair. Unable to walk or stand most of the time, Robert finds it difficult to use public transport and instead drives into work using an adapted car with hand levers rather than pedals. His firm provides a parking space and he uses a manual wheelchair to get from the front to the back of his car where he assembles his power chair for use around the offices.

Robert is now aged 47 (39 when he first fell ill) and trained and qualified at Hogan Lovells. Despite his illness, Robert wanted to continue working in his firm's litigation sector, which he now does as a professional support lawyer. Robert describes his firm as 'a good place to work – definitely employee-friendly. This is important for everyone, but particularly for those who need to work flexibly, as I do, if they are to continue their career.'

Practicalities

Currently Robert works three days in the office and two days from his office at home. On the days he works in London, his basic hours are 10.30 to 18.30, which enable him to drive into work and avoid the worst of the rush hour traffic. He varies which days he is in the office so he can attend meetings and other events on any day of the week, but because most people contact him by email or phone (which can be diverted), 'most people I deal with don't know whether I am working in the office or from home.'

Robert's condition varies, but he always has to be careful to minimise physical exertion.

> My current mix of working from my office at home and my office in the City allows me to do this, with the benefit of recent technological developments and excellent support from my firm's IT department. For instance, we have a good remote working system, which enables employees to log on to emails and databases from whatever location they happen to be in, and I've been given a first class laser printer which I can keep within arm's reach of my desk in my office at home and use to print large documents just as if I were in my office in London.

Reducing the number of days he has to commute into work, and changing his hours so he can travel by car rather than public transport, helps Robert conserve his energy and manage his symptoms without compromising the amount or intensity of the work he takes on. Fee earning work was not possible when he was confined to his bed, and would probably not be practical now because of the need to visit the court, clients and witnesses on a regular basis, but there are no limits to what he can do in his present 'in-house' role.

CASE STUDY: Part-time working

Context and background

As a legal director with Pinsent Masons, one of the biggest national law firms, Jane is 18 years' PQE and a commercial property specialist and legal director. Pinsent Masons introduced the legal director role three years ago, as an alternative career path to partnership. Legal directors attend partners meetings and take an active role in the management and development of the business.

Shifting attitudes: flexible working is a business issue

Jane opted to work flexibly following the birth of her third child in 2002. At that point she worked for a different law firm, and the first flexible working legislation had been introduced.

> Asking for flexible working was not really acceptable then, so my request was greeted with a sharp intake of breath.

At that point, a three-day week was not considered possible but four days was agreed to. Jane started working flexibly when no firms offered either the technical capability or possibility to work flexibly, including from home.

Four years ago, Jane was recruited back to Pinsent Masons (where she had originally worked). Since then, much has changed and it is much more acceptable to ask for flexible working. However, Jane reflects that being a senior professional will always bring more autonomy to working flexibly, acknowledging that this may not be the case for more junior lawyers, 'however there are many more women working flexibly now, others here have very flexible arrangements.'

Practicalities and challenges of working flexibly

Jane currently works four days and whatever else her role requires, which can include weekends where matters arise.

> When I am in the office, I am extremely focused on what I have to do – although I work normal office hours, I am flexible and do whatever I need to do to which may include working weekends at times.
>
> With a family, evenings are busy, so I come in early.
>
> Having time boundaries as a lawyer is a key challenge, as well as proving your commitment. As lawyers, we are innately conscientious, so it is hard if you are very busy and have to leave the office. It can make you feel like a slacker, even though I know I will pick up my work again in the evening or come in really early.

What would you advise other people considering working flexibly?

> The main thing is to be open about your working practices with clients – so that you can effectively manage their expectations. My clients know that I am not in the office on Fridays but will be if needed. The other key factor is highly focused time management. Having time boundaries actually makes you more efficient and focused, other colleagues have commented on me being 'incredibly efficient'. This is because as a lawyer working flexibly, you are very driven and committed to be very organised, flexible and highly effective in your role.

Alternative roles to the partner track for senior lawyers

Through introducing this role, Pinsent Masons have responded to the fact that not all of their top lawyers want to pursue the partnership track (and accompanying life choices). This role was developed in recognition of the fact that not all of the best lawyers aspire to partnership but do want challenging work and to achieve professional excellence. This initiative has proved an effective measure and is reducing/stopping the 'talent drain' of senior associates. Jane was in the first tier to be made up to legal director, three years ago at Pinsent Masons.

> Law firms have woken up to the need to keep people – they are addressing this as a significant business issue, not as an HR or diversity issue. This is important.

At the same time, she acknowledges that:

> ... we are still in a transition – there are still people who may see you as less committed, if you work flexibly. But year on year that view is being diluted.

Today Jane takes part in partner meetings and plays an active role in the management of the business.

> I made a clear decision not to go for partnership – I made an active choice away from unpredictable hours.

These case studies illustrate that flexible working can and is being seen in the legal sector. But to work flexibly in a law firm is not without its challenges.

Key points from the case studies include:

- Be flexible – sometimes you may need to change your days.
- Be careful in your choice of job share partner – make sure you are a good fit.
- Partnership may not be the only way to progress your legal career.
- Managing client expectations is critical to success.
- Remote working requires dedication and great IT systems.

Chapter 11

Changing direction: careers outside the law

Ruth Fenton

Introduction

This chapter is designed to assist people looking for an alternative career that utilises skills developed while studying or practising law. It covers the following areas:

- How you decide on an alternative career path and create your dream job.
- The transferable skills which will help you obtain and be successful in your new role.
- The careers that utilise the transferable skills legal professionals have.
- How you can find out more about alternative careers.
- Examples of people who have made a successful transition from law to an alternative career.
- Seven steps to landing your next job.

How do you decide on an alternative career path?

Have you ever asked yourself why you wanted to study law? The first thing that comes into your head might not be the real reason behind your decision. It could be a non-job related reason, for example, you wanted to earn lots of money or a job related reason, such as you wanted to assist people using the law to resolve their disputes. As we spend a massive portion of our time at work, it is important to do something we love, feel fulfilled by and can thrive in. When people are fulfilled they tend to be more successful. Having a non-job related reason for embarking on a career may ultimately mean we are not fulfilled.

There are many reasons why people consider changing career, for example, redundancy, medical reasons, boredom, wanting a better work/life balance, family circumstance, wanting more or less responsibility, needing a new challenge, etc. If we are not happy in our work, our personal life and health can be impacted.

Starting out in a new job or career can be daunting but knowing we have made the right decision from day one will help us build confidence and

119

motivate us to follow our goals. When considering changing direction it is worth considering the financial and emotional impact it will create both for you and the significant people around you.

Consider the following:

- *Family and personal commitments:* Do you need to fit your job around childcare, caring for someone or a non-work related activity?
- *Location:* Will you need to relocate? Will this adversely impact on your social network and family?
- *Financial circumstances:* If you are looking at a career that pays less than your current job, can you meet your current financial commitments and pay for any additional expenses you might incur? Will you need to retrain in your own time and at your own expense?
- *Current employment status:* How urgently do you need to change? Is your current job safe or do you need to escape quickly? If you are unemployed, are you entitled to any benefits while you look for work?
- *Timing:* How long might it take to find something new? What is your back up plan if things do not work out how you expect?
- *Restrictions on employment:* Do you have a criminal record or visa conditions preventing you working in certain sectors or for certain employers? Or do you need a certain qualification or certificate?

Dream job creator

The following short exercise is a fun way of discovering what you really want from a job and your career.

1. The mind map in **Figure 11.1** highlights the key headings you should consider when creating your dream job. When writing down, for example, what hours you would like to work, also write down why. It may be after carefully thinking about the real reason behind your idea, you would like to change it. At this point, you do not need to have a specific role or career in mind. Think of it this way: maps are useless unless you know where you are. Knowing what you want will put you on the map so you can then move towards your specific job goal.
2. Now you have your dream job in mind you can start matching it to industries and professions which will fulfil your criteria. A list of possible careers are suggested later in this chapter. It is useful to speak to people who are already doing the job to see whether it is something you would enjoy doing and to find out more about it.
3. Starting with the end in mind, what's your outcome? Considering both a professional and personal outcome will help you balance your work and personal life and allow you to resolve any conflicts between the two before you embark on a new career. This should also help you to make

better informed choices. Entering a new life stage, for example becoming a parent, often makes people re-evaluate what is really important to them in their personal life and career.

4. Consider your motive to be your rocket fuel. If you have the right reasons to want to do it and you are 100 per cent committed, you will find a way to make it happen as opportunities will become clearer. Knowing the why will give you the how.

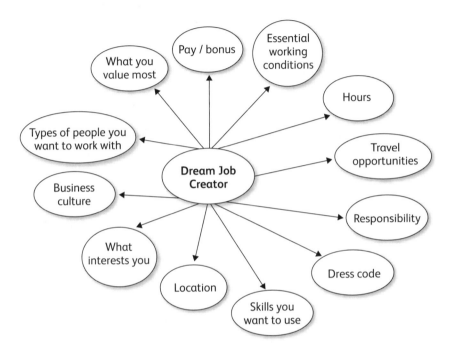

Figure 11.1 Dream job creator: suggested areas to consider when planning your move

Transferable skills

Law students and lawyers are very fortunate that they acquire a whole range of transferrable skills which makes a career transition much easier. Once you have an idea of the type of job in which you are interested, you can start matching your skills to the skills required by the job. It is then possible to see where you may need further training, experience or information before committing to changing career.

Skills sheet exercise

Create a skills sheet listing all the transferable skills you have and how strong they are, when you obtained them and how you are working on improving them. This will allow you to pick and mix the necessary skills when completing application forms and match them to a particular role. In interviews employers often want to know where you obtained your skills so they can gauge whether you will need additional training.

Table 11.1 An example of how to set out the skills sheet

Skill	Where acquired	Date	Example	How to develop it further
Present-ing (basic)	Speakers Academy	16.10.2009	Public speaking in front of 100 people	Coaching and practice
	Law Firm A	20.03.2007	Advocacy in court	Mock trials

Below is a list of skills that legal professionals commonly develop. This is a good starting point for creating your own personalised list.

Intellectual skills
- Gathering, comparing, contrasting, and combining information and data.
- Researching via a wide range of information resources.
- Remembering facts and figures.
- Paying attention to detail and checking for accuracy.
- Thinking critically.

Interpersonal skills
- Effectively communicating complex ideas.
- Establishing and maintaining effective relationships.
- Being sensitive to others' views and concerns.
- Listening, interviewing, negotiating and persuading.
- Creating reasoned conclusions.
- Presenting.

Organisational skills
- Time management.
- Working under pressure.
- Coordinating work.

- Setting priorities and balancing competing needs.
- Keeping parties and colleagues up to date with progress.

Creative skills
- Problem solving.
- Creating opportunities.
- Lateral thinking.

Technical skills
- Commercial awareness.
- Understanding business risks and liabilities.
- Translating technical legal concepts in to plain English.
- Drafting documents.
- Proofreading.
- Computing/IT.

Personal attributes
- Professionalism.
- Determination.
- Commitment to learning and self-development.

Other skills such as team working, managing people and resources may need further development especially amongst junior lawyers and law students. It is also good to know where your weaknesses are so you can build on them, especially if they are required for your new career.

Not only do legal professionals have transferable skills, they also have experiences and knowledge, which can be very beneficial to other organisations. Creating a mind map or listing your knowledge and experience will help you when tailoring applications. Listing all your achievements will foster confidence and put you in a positive frame of mind.

CASE STUDY: Solicitor to legal business strategist

Prior to becoming a solicitor I worked as a business consultant advising small businesses in the UK and overseas. At university I studied BA (Hons) Business and Law and went on to study the Legal Practice Course (LPC). I worked for a number of years as a paralegal at two magic circle law firms before obtaining a training contract and ultimately qualifying as a solicitor. In 2010 I became a mother. Due to my financial circumstances, I had to find work to pay my mortgage. Being in the middle of the recession, it was impossible to find any part-time work in my legal field of expertise, so I started to look for opportunities outside of the law. Setting up my own business seemed a logical thing to do. It meant my hours were flexible and fit around my children.

I have been able to combine my legal, business and psychology skills and knowledge to set up a niche coaching practice aimed at legal professionals. As a legal business strategist, my legal training has been invaluable as I understand the pressures and challenges lawyers and law firms face in the current economic climate. I use many of the legal skills I have picked up along the way, for example, accounting, presenting, setting up a company, listening, problem solving, attention to detail, etc. The work is extremely rewarding and fits in very well with my personal circumstances.

Alternatives to being a solicitor or barrister

Table 11.2   Alternative careers where a legal background would be very beneficial

Home Office	Foreign Office	Paralegal	Serious Fraud Office
Ministry of Justice	Legal executive	Will writer	Local authority – housing and environmental departments
HM Revenue and Customs	UK Border Agency	Stockbroker	Insurance claims handler
Court clerk	Legal recruitment	Expert witness	European Commission
Legal case worker	Chartered secretary	Editor	Teaching/academic
Law librarian	Diplomatic service	Coroner	Police station representation
Company director	MI5/MI6	Outdoor clerk	Compliance officer/ Policy maker
Patent agent	Costs draftsman	Customer services	Corporate negotiator
Accountant	Tax advisor	Technical writer	Management consultant
Medical ethics	Politics	Sports agent	Registrar of Births, Deaths and Marriages
Bailiff	Banking	Tipstaff	Trade mark attorney
Heir hunter	Legal journalist	Legal IT	Office of Fair Trading
Mediator	Business coach	Probation service	Insurance underwriter
Military	Victim support	Legal outsourcing	Charities, e.g. Amicus
Equity and Human Rights Commission	Jury consultant (USA)	Marriage guidance counsellor	Business development
Political advisor	Forensic accountant	Private investigator	Civil enforcement officer

Retail nego-tiator	Conveyancer	Litigation friend	Security industry authority
TV researcher	Police	United Nations	Citizens advice bureau

CASE STUDY: LPC student to insurance underwriter

At university I studied a fine art valuation degree and subsequently went on to do the Common Professional Examination (CPE) and LPC at Bournemouth University. Despite numerous applications I was unsuccessful in trying to find myself a training contract. Disillusioned, I found myself working in London in the high net worth claims department of a respected insurance company. Around six months later, the opportunity arose for me to work as an underwriter in the financial lines area of the business. I was suitable due to my legal qualifications and the nature of the insurable risks. These centred on directors' and officers' liabilities. I worked in this area for around 10 years, gaining a lot of experience in identifying legal exposures arising out of a company's activities.

More recently, the above experience has enabled me to move into the legal expenses area of insurance and now I work with partner law firms to create products either for the insurance company I work for, or bespoke products for affinity clients. It's an interesting role and one which I can directly attribute to my decision to study law.

Information sources

Before you start applying for jobs, it is worth finding out more about the trade or profession you would like to enter. Listed below are several services that may be useful to you.

- The National Careers Service (**https://nationalcareers service.direct. gov.uk**) provides a comprehensive list of different job profiles which is a good starting point when considering a different career. There are also various career questionnaires on the internet where you answer questions and they then match your personal attributes and skills to suggest possible careers you might be interested in.
- Trade directories will provide lists of businesses within a certain sector which you can approach to find out more. The companies may be ranked so you know who the market leaders are for that sector.
- Professional bodies will be able to provide information on qualifications needed, rules, policies and how the profession is regulated and governed.
- Trade organisations will be able to provide a snapshot of the industry and how it is developing. They may also run seminars and training and have a trade publication you can subscribe to.

- Specialist recruitment agents should be able to give you the low down on the career you are considering along with average salaries and the types of skills, qualifications and experience you will need.
- Market research databases, for example Mintel, provide industry reports noting consumer trends, product innovations and market trends. Having knowledge of the annual reports and industry statistics will be great talking points at the interview.

By now you should have a good idea of your dream job. Ideally you should have a list of five to 10 organisations which fit your goals and interest you. If you are unsure which organisations to approach, the activities below should help you narrow down your search to focus on the right ones for you.

Seven steps to landing your next job

1. Networking

It's not what you know, it's who you know. Networking is a great way to give you a competitive advantage over other applicants. The job market is extremely competitive so making a good impression in front of the right people is critical. Using business psychology to build a rapport should quickly impress potential employers. It's not so much what you say, but how you make the other person feel when you are talking to them. If they come away from the conversation feeling like you care about what they do and you're keen to learn more, they are more likely to help you. Remember to always follow up with an email or phone call the same day to thank them for their time and ask any additional questions.

Avenues for networking include the following:

- *Find a mentor in an area in which you want to specialise.* Having a mentor can fast track you to success. Mentors are able to share mistakes that they made so you don't need to make them yourself. Mentors will often have contacts and can offer advice on how to get ahead. They may know of people recruiting and, if you make a good impression, can recommend you for positions. Of course you can have more than one mentor to support you and increase your chances of finding that dream job. Modelling success will help you to become successful.
- *Attend client webinars and seminars.* Many businesses have client newsletters and free webinars. Signing up for an area which interests you will keep you up to date on the latest developments. This can be a good conversation point at interview. If available, attend an open day or client seminars. This is a great way to meet people in an informal way and express your interest in finding out more. Writing something about the person on his or her business card should help you remember the conversation you had.

- *Use family and business contacts to introduce you to prospective employers.* Given two equal candidates, HR is more likely to pick someone for interview who has shown an interest and made an effort to find out more about the business. Pick up the phone and talk to employees in the business you want to work for. Make sure you do your homework on them first: Google them, check their CV, etc. so you know exactly with whom you are talking. If you can get a referral from someone else, this is great as an opening line. It's also a great way of getting past the secretary 'gatekeeper'. Have a 30-second personal pitch ready to get them curious and invite them for a coffee to discuss further. Once you have met them, at the end of the conversation ask if there is someone else who could provide a different view of the organisation.
- *Attend trade events in an area of business you are interested in.* Get to know the main players in the sector so you have something to talk about at the interview. This will increase your awareness and get you in front of the right people.
- *Join groups of interest.* Get involved on committees, for example within trade associations.
- *Use social networking sites.* For example, LinkedIn, Ecademy, Xing, etc. LinkedIn has a number of different business interest groups you can join. This is a great way to make contacts and find out more about potential careers. It will also raise your profile to get testimonials from people you have worked with in the past so they appear on your LinkedIn page. LinkedIn has a section where you can put key skills so when people are searching for a person with particular expertise you are more likely to come up. Find and use contacts of friends and family who may be useful to your search. Be aware that employers commonly look you up on Facebook so it's advisable to either not post anything you would not like them to see or make your profile private.

2. Business intelligence

When looking at career alternatives, it is important to know what is going on within the business sector or profession.

Career fairs are a great way to gather information about companies and speak directly to HR professionals. Remember to dress smartly and take your CV with you. Researching the companies which are attending the fair beforehand and creating intelligent questions will make you stand out from others. A good way to research them is by looking at their websites and any press stories.

Every business is different although you will find some similarities across sectors. Being realistic about the hours and working conditions you would like is very important. Consider the support the business will offer. Will you get training, a secretary, and have things organised for you, etc.? A career change may be perfect for you but in the wrong business culture, it could be very challenging. It may help to check out the diversity policy and statistics which are sometimes published on a business' website.

Recruitment agents may be able to give you some valuable insights into certain companies or sector areas. Agents may have good contacts to help you get an interview even if the company is not recruiting at that moment.

3. Work experience

If you are changing careers your prospective employers will need to know you are 100 per cent committed to the change before they start spending lots of money on additional training if needed. Having work experience, either paid or unpaid, will show your commitment and help you decide if the career move is right for you.

Gaining additional training and qualifications in your chosen field should assist you, but always check their value before committing a lot of time and money. It may be an employer offers a training scheme or apprenticeship whereby they pay for additional courses and training.

4. Standing out

Businesses are looking for candidates who stand out, who have contacts and are business minded. The switched-on businesses will be succession planning and looking for candidates who will grow the business, improve the quality and stay with them.

Think about the following:

- With whom do you need to network to get potential clients for them?
- How can you learn more about their business world?
- How can you best demonstrate the skills and knowledge that you have in a way which is beneficial to their business?
- How can you get your name known? For example, having articles published in trade journals and speaking at trade events is a great way to get your name known (even if you just ask the speaker an intelligent question).

An excellent way to stand out is by writing a business case. Once you have gathered information about a prospective employer and researched the company and industry, you will be able to write a business case noting transferable skills and expertise you can bring to the organisation and how you can help it grow and develop to become even more successful. Creating a business case may also help you get an interview where currently there is no position on offer.

5. Filling in application forms

This is where your transferable skills table and knowledge come into their own. Not only will it help you create a tailored CV and covering letter, it will also assist you in your interview.

When applying for a role look carefully at the job description and match your relevant skills and knowledge to it. It's a good idea to look at job descriptions from a number of companies with the same sort of roles to see the common skills and experience they are asking for. This will give you more of an idea of what is out there and how roles may slightly differ depending on the business. For example, a sales manager role in one company may use face-to-face selling and another telephone selling – same role but slightly different skill sets.

If you know someone within the business who will sing your praises, mention them. Many companies have an employee incentive scheme which means if an employee introduces a candidate to the business and the candidate is ultimately employed with the business for a certain amount of time, the employee often gets cash for saving the business recruitment costs. Plus recruiters are more likely to go with someone who is recommended by a current employee.

Remember to mention the business contacts you have and those employees with whom you networked, why you stand out from others and niche areas of expertise. If you get invited to interview you could also present a business case as mentioned above. This shows you have done your homework and are totally committed to joining their business.

Make sure you follow up with interested businesses and obtain feedback if you are unsuccessful. Where there are lots of people going for the same job it is sometimes possible to get an interview even if you have been rejected at the first stage just by showing tenacity. Sometimes HR electronically search keywords within a CV so you might be rejected if the computer fails to pick up the keywords, even though you have the right experience and skills.

Reward yourself for progress. It can be soul destroying when you make lots of applications and don't hear back or you are unsuccessful. Remember, with every phone call and application you make you are one step closer to that dream job. Make the application process fun, for example, play your favourite music or draft the application forms in your favourite location. Investing in your future will lead to a more fulfilled life.

6. Feedback

Write down the names of all the companies you apply to, the date, the name of the person, his or her email address and phone number, where a copy of your application can be found, the outcome and details of any conversations and feedback you received. Why? It sounds like a lot of work but it will help you no end when you have made a number of applications. It's so easy to forget to whom you have applied and what was said, especially if you are unsuccessful as you just want to forget about it. You can also add links to the companies' information to save you from researching it twice. Having your own personal database will help you identify which companies are recruiting without going through agents. Where you do use agents they will want to know with whom you have applied so they don't put you forward for the same roles.

Phone for feedback (emails are easier to ignore). Really listen to what they are telling you, change future applications and get the experience you need. Think about how you are going to measure your successes. Remember, the biggest lessons often come from when things have not turned out how you would like. Learn from your mistakes and build on what you did well. Share your experiences with others, as they might share something which can help you avoid making the same mistake and can help you get an interview.

7. Backup strategy

You may have one career move in mind but it doesn't work out how you expect or you struggle to find what you are looking for. In the current economic climate it's helpful to have an answer to the following questions:

- Who will support you in your quest?
- When will you know it's time to change tactics?
- If things don't go your way, what is your backup plan?

If things don't work out at first, you may need to ask better questions to get the answers you require. A chance conversation or meeting can transform your career so perseverance and determination is key.

Having a support network is very important. Some people find having a coach to support them very beneficial. Coaches can help keep you motivated and on target with applications and research. Once you start a new job, the business culture, unfamiliar work and new people to work with can be challenging in the first few weeks. Having a support network can help you develop new skills and overcome initial challenges.

Conclusion

In this chapter we have covered what you should consider when looking to change career and how you should go about finding your dream job. Having completed the dream job creator and skills sheet exercises, you should now be in a much stronger position to make targeted, focused applications.

The seven steps to landing your next job covered how having a mentor and networking greatly increase your chances of securing a role, and how the transferable skills law professionals already have make transitioning into an alternative career much easier. Additionally, they covered how obtaining work experience and business intelligence will make you stand out as a candidate and acting on feedback will make your applications stronger. Finally, having a backup plan is highly advisable along with a support network.

Changing direction can provide exciting opportunities for a rewarding career outside of the law so whether your circumstances are forcing action, or you just fancy a change, you have a wealth of options available.

Appendix A

Changing career direction or changing from one practice area to another

The following is an edited transcript of a session held at the Junior Lawyers Division annual conference on 27 April 2013. It reflects a concern that junior lawyers are specialising increasingly early in their careers and that it can be difficult to move into another practice area thereafter. The speakers were Linda Lee, a former President of the Law Society; Nigel Gardner, a partner at national law firm DWF; and Michelle Penn, a Law Society council member and partner at Berrymans Lace Mawer.

Linda Lee

My career changes have been brought about by necessity. I trained in a firm which did trade union work and particularly mining, which I enjoyed. However just after I qualified, the mining industry collapsed and it became clear that that career path wasn't sustainable. Therefore, I thought, 'What can I do? What skills do I have?' I liked medical negligence work, but the firm did not specialise in this area. Therefore I put together a business plan which I put to the firm. I asked them to let me train in this area of work and I would develop it for them. And this is what I did.

I then moved to a bigger firm and again developed the clinical negligence practice. I then moved in-house. When I was looking to move in-house I realised that I did not have the commercial skills which are necessary for that sector. I then had to ask myself what skills did I have? I had a reputation as a medical negligence practitioner so I moved to a medical negligence charity. I was then elected President of the Law Society, which was a terrific honour, but it meant that I lost my medical negligence accreditation. It meant that, realistically, I could not go back to doing claimant medical negligence work unless I built up a portfolio of cases, which would have taken me six years. I could have moved to defendant medical negligence work but my heart was not in this and thus out of necessity I had to change again.

I therefore moved to regulatory work. Because of my role as President of the Law Society, being a Law Society council member and sitting on various committees and Boards, I had already been very involved with regulatory matters and this is what I am doing now.

I have to say that there is something quite fascinating about changing career direction, although it is daunting. But once you are in a new area of work, it revives your interest in the law.

So how do you go about it?

1.   If you are in a training contract get as much experience as possible. In some

firms you are allocated different seats but I see people choosing very similar ones. Get as much experience as you can – and in a broad variety of areas.

2. If you are newly qualified and thinking of changing you need to do some research. It is easier to change in the first few years after qualification than when you are older and much longer qualified. However you are young in your professional careers and thus more attractive to an employer looking to take on someone seeking a career change.

What research do you need to do?

1. Ask yourself, what skills do I have? Make a ruthless self-assessment of yourself. What interests do you have? What skills are allied to where you want to be? Do you plan to go into an area already overcrowded or collapsing? Find, if you can, something where there is a realistic possibility for growth, or at least not shrinkage in the market.

2. What suits your personality? My daughter, who is a solicitor, qualified in 2011. She moved from a legal aid firm to being an army legal adviser. However she had done family and criminal work while in private practice and these are areas of work which have put her in good stead in the army. Find something that suits you.

3. If you are already in a law firm is there scope in your existing firm to change? Can you persuade them to support you in a new practice area? Have they a department doing the work you want to do? If not, might they like to create one? However if they agree to train you, and pay for that training, how are you going to repay them? What sort of business plan can you put forward? Where are you going to get clients from? How can you prove you can do the work and make it profitable? You might think that you are at an early stage of your career to be doing that but it is never too early. Probably your best years as a lawyer are when you are newly qualified and enthusiastic. You are likely to achieve more than someone saying, begrudgingly, I have been doing this for 10 years and I suppose I had better change. Thus look at the positive aspects but think how you are going to sell it to the firm.

4. If you can't retrain within your firm and are thus looking to develop outside the organisation, how are you going to increase your skills? Look at the area you want to be in. Is there a professional association already set up? Join it as a junior member, attend its courses, network and consider doing pro bono work in that area. Build on your existing skills. Go on courses, paying for them yourself if your firm won't pay. It may seem like a big ask but it is an investment in your future.

I have recruited people to work in medical negligence at a junior level who are not specialists. At any interview for a career change you need to prove you are keen, have done your research and can show what steps you have taken. Make sure that the firm understands that you are someone willing to learn and not already set in your ways and views.

I interviewed one particular young solicitor for a position who asked how long they would have to work in my team before they could transfer to another area of work in the firm. This is not a good approach.

You are going to need to identify the skills which are needed. The latest Law Society annual statistical report has just been published and in some respects it makes grim reading. What is clear is that there is an increased number of solicitors with practicing certificates who are not attached to any particular organisation who are qualified and out there looking for work. It is a desperate state of affairs because while the number of people in this situation is increasing, the opportunities in lots of areas are shrinking. However, you can't be too disheartened. It may be difficult moving to a new practice area but somebody has to succeed. Why shouldn't that be you?

Nigel Gardner

I practice in non-contentious commercial law and intellectual property in a large national law firm. I have been doing this for over 10 years.

My journey has been as follows. I trained in a city firm and qualified in 1991. However at that time I didn't want to stay in the law and so I went off and did non-law related work in publishing and television. Eventually I decided I wanted to go back into law and I thus secured a position working in-house for the BBC. I had already been working for the BBC as a researcher and various related jobs and it seemed like a natural progression and combination of what I had been broadly interested in such as television, media, and IP. I was thus able to marry the two. I worked mainly on contracting artists for programmes like Casualty and EastEnders, which in turn, was a useful transition back into private practice.

For various domestic reasons I needed to relocate to the Midlands which is where I am now. It also suited me at the time of the move to go back into private practice. I ended up doing corporate work but not sure how, probably because there weren't many opportunities to do media and entertainment work in the Midlands at that time. The firm took a chance on me, coming from in-house back into private practice and in a different area of work. My sense is it was a lot easier to transfer between different practice areas than it is now.

So I was doing corporate mergers and acquisitions work for a few years. But I wasn't really into the culture of that type of work. I was more interested in drafting and negotiating contracts, preferably with some sort of IP or media and entertainment bent, and dealing with people than in dealing with banks and corporations on mergers and acquisitions. I didn't want to be a corporate lawyer long term, so what did I want to do?

I spoke to a partner in my firm responsible for drafting and negotiating contracts and asked whether I could join his team. I cultivated a relationship with him. It probably took me about 18 months to make the transition from corporate to commercial. I did quite a broad range of commercial work in that it wasn't very niche. I covered all sorts of work from supply contracts and licensing contracts to joint ventures and entertainment projects. I made that decision and it worked for me. I have done and continue to do that type of work for the last 10 years and I really enjoy it.

I was fortunate to be able to change my practice area albeit I had a plan and I prepared accordingly. However, because of the current state of the economy it is much more difficult to do now what I did back then. Firms like mine now tend to look internally and use their own trained staff to retrain before they look at external candidates. Furthermore, even internal candidates may be expected to have done a seat in the practice area into which they want to move, or have experience in a similar area. I mention this because I think it is probably in the commercial and corporate world as difficult now as it has ever been to change practice areas.

While that is true you shouldn't feel deflated. The skills you will need to successfully transition from, say employment to corporate, are essentially the same. If you are assiduous and dedicated and do all the things Linda mentioned above, for example, researching what's out there and getting experience, even on a pro bono basis, the opportunities are still there. The realities of the modern law firm are this – if people like your enthusiasm, like what you bring 'to the party' so to speak, you are going to have a look in. If you are the kind of person who can demonstrate that you are committed, innovative, know your way around and can show why you have a case then there are opportunities there. But be aware, it is a very competitive landscape.

However, you cannot afford to shirk on the preparation you need to do if you were to put yourself in front of someone like me, for example, and say 'I know I have been doing this particular area of work for a few years but I would now like to change'. You really have to build up a case as to why the change can and will work for you. It is difficult. However, if I see that glint in your eye, clear passion for the work, demonstration of your skills and ability to work well, and good references from people you have worked with, both in business and externally, then there will be an opportunity.

Finally, build up a portfolio of skills to use and sell yourself to an employer. Whether you are staying in a practice area or changing, think about what sets you apart from your peers, so when you change areas or seek to progress your career you can present yourself as having distinctive features.

Michelle Penn

I qualified at the age of 32 and have been a partner at Berrymans Lace Mawer (BLM) since 2003, although I have been with the firm since 2000. I specialise in disease work and I have being doing this since 1995. My story is about going from general practitioner in personal injury to a specialist niche area and then going from claimant work to defendant.

I started my training at the Crown Prosecution Service but as you can't stay there for the whole of your training period, as it is only one practice area, I therefore went on secondment to a legal aid firm and qualified there. But they didn't really specialise in personal injury work in the way I would have liked. A job opportunity then came up at Thompsons, a large union law firm, where I stayed for five years. I really loved my time there but things moved on and due to changes in the management structure I didn't think I had much of a future there, albeit that is where I started to specialise in disease claims, partly because at that time the unions were involved in getting their members much more aware of disease-type claims, particularly repetitive strain injury and stress.

In about 2000 I had a complex case involving anaphylactic shock. I got heavily involved with BLM who were on the other side. Eventually my CV landed on their desk and I ended up going into partnership there, which is where I am now. And that is what I do. I specialise. One of the key things for me is specialisation and finding a niche area.

Most of the people I recruit have never had any experience of defendant work or disease work. But that doesn't necessarily matter. But I do agree with Linda. If you want to make those moves and become a specialist, whether it is in claimant or defendant work, you do so at an early stage of your career.

I interview lots of different people. Disease work tends to be a growing area, partly because claimant solicitors are always looking for creative ways of making work profitable and disease is still more profitable than, say personal injury. When I am looking to recruit it is great if candidates have experience in the area, but that is not all that I am looking for. I am looking for someone who is keen, enthusiastic and actually has an awareness of the area of law. If I am interviewing someone for a disease position I want to know that they have looked me up on the BLM website and found out what I do, what the firm does and what disease work involves. There is nothing worse than asking somebody why they are interested in being a disease lawyer and they just have that vacant look. They may end up being a really fantastic person to take on but unless they can show me an interest in that area of law, they won't make a favourable impression.

The interview is a very blunt instrument when you're trying to find the right person, which is why we do tend to take on trainees in newly qualified positions, as Nigel mentioned, as you have basically interviewed them over a two-year process and they may have spent six months with you. So when you are just coming for an interview and spending 45 minutes to an hour with someone who has seen only your CV, try to impress on that person that you really want to work for them. If you have not invested your time in finding out who is interviewing you, what he or she does and what his or her specialisation is, it is a wasted opportunity.

The other thing is, and I know this from claimant and defendant work, if you are involved in litigation you want good people on both sides. I know when Linda was President of the Law Society I heard her say on many occasions in council meetings the words 'access to justice' and it was always said in terms of acting for claimants. However, if you have the right person on both sides you give the claimant access to justice, because you make the right decision as early as possible which can include settling the claim, and also giving access to justice to the defendant. Defendants are not always big faceless corporate clients. Sometimes they are very small businesses and a claim against them can cause a great deal of stress. Because I defend about 50 per cent of the claims I am involved with it suggests that things aren't always the 'claimant is right and the defendant is wrong'. There is lots of grey in between – we all know that. I think as lawyers we should always be able to act for claimants or defendants and always feel that what we are doing is in the best interests of our clients and access to justice.

And once again talking about specialisation, I think the key thing for me is to make sure that whoever seeks legal advice gets specialist legal advice. When you act for the defendant it is a 'given' because you are acting for an insurance company and are likely to be on an approved panel. Claimants are different. On the whole when they go to a union firm they will have access to a specialist but quite often they won't and I am often up against all types of lawyers who do not have experience in this area. I am very much of the view that access to justice is also about claimants finding a specialist lawyer and I am working with the Law Society on the possible development of an accreditation scheme for disease work lawyers. It is not the complete answer but it is a step in the right direction.

Questions and answers

Q1: I am sure you are all aware that when you come to the end of your training contract you are faced with a make or break decision about what you need to specialise in. That isn't always based on what you are interested in or what you have been exposed to. It is often based on capacity and vacancies within firms. So my question is, would you recommend taking a risk and face unemployment by holding out to do what you want to do by waiting for that opportunity, or take a position in your firm because there is a vacancy and then cross into another practice area when the opportunity arises?

Linda: I am from the North of England and at the time when I grew up there were people who had never had jobs and have never worked. Therefore the idea of taking time off and not working is abhorrent to me. I can justify it from a practical response which is, if you have got a job it is better to go from a job to another job. Although I have made changes in my career, I have never got exactly what I wanted. I always got to the nearest place I could get to and never had too fixed an idea of what I wanted. I would advise therefore that you look at developing your skills to where you want to go to and take whatever job you can get. If it is a job or no job – take the job. And then, over a period of time, you can work to where you want to be. Constantly reassess that. Is that really where you want to be or might you find that where you are now is quite good? No, don't take time out.

Michelle: In this market if there is a job you take it. Carry on getting your experience. Look elsewhere but the grass isn't always greener. If you are happy with where you are, stay there. The trouble with lawyers is that we tend to be very ambitious and driven, which is great, but there may be opportunities where you are already working. Take the job opportunity.

Nigel: Not because I disagree with Linda or Michelle, but to give you a different view, it obviously depends upon your circumstances. If you can afford not to take the job and do something which would be more stimulating or rewarding for you, then it is a slightly different scenario from someone who financially or emotionally cannot afford to be out work for a period of time. But you are not alone. There are lots of people in my firm who had the same challenge because the vacancies weren't necessarily in the areas they wanted but they made an evaluation and said, well at least I am in the firm I want to be in working with people I like and I will either get to like this area or I will be in the front row to move to where I want to go. It may make that path easier if I stay where I am.

Q2:   One of the points I picked up was what Linda said about getting as broad experience as possible when you are a trainee. Is there not a risk that once you come to qualifying and want to go into a particular area, the team you hope to work in might consider that your very broad experience is too diluted in terms of the skills set you can offer?

Linda: My view is you will need as broad a base as possible and one of the reasons I am not keen on accreditation schemes, which we have had in clinical negligence for a long time, is that it compels people to specialise too soon and that doesn't really develop them as lawyers. They will be perfect at doing a limited range of claims but as lawyers they lose something. When you are newly qualified you are young in professional terms and you don't know what is out there in the legal world. You will restrict your chances. I know it is not always possible given the way some firms are structured but I don't think you can ever fail to benefit from having as broad an experience as possible. I really wish I had done more non-contentious work in my training contract. I kept that to a minimum because I loathed it but I wish as a lawyer I had increased my understanding of it.

Michelle: I agree. At BLM we ensure that a trainee has their four lots of six months' seat rotation during the training contract. Even if we want to keep somebody it is important that they have a broad range of experience in contentious and non-contentious work and have done a variety of work. You make your choices so that when the vacancies come up you know where you want to go or have a better idea about it. Don't ever lose that opportunity of getting that experience. If a firm wants to take you on, give you a training contract or give you experience in different areas, don't let it pass you by. You may never have those opportunities again.

Nigel: No self-respecting law firm is going to write off its own trainees on the basis that they don't have broad enough training experience. It undermines their own practice and training provision. So it shouldn't be a scenario you are faced with. But if you are it could be because of the way the legal world is developing and the training contract is itself becoming more specialised. It is sad but a reality, particularly in commercial firms. There is now a trend where firms looking to qualify their trainees into a particular team will expect them to do about 12 months of the training contract in that seat, as they like you to spend time there and for it to be your final seat. It means you don't necessarily get the broad base training, which is a shame. However not all firms are structured this way.

Q3: Nigel, as well as moving between practice areas you also mentioned in-house work. For those of us thinking about that, what are your thoughts about doing so in the current climate or the transferability if you want to move back again?

Nigel: You might want to speak to recruitment consultants about this. When I was speaking with them recently I kept being told that the journey or path from private practice to in-house is now well trodden. It is very much the 'in thing'. A lot of solicitors want to go into in-house roles because they haven't necessarily enjoyed their experience in private practice and see the overall package of in-house work as more attractive, for example, in terms of the salary, the work life balance and giving one more freedom than private practice. It is very hot right now with a lot of in-house jobs being advertised – but it is also creating competition between private practice solicitors to go into those roles. Making the journey back into private practice is equally hot. A lawyer with in-house experience can be an attractive prospect for those seeking to recruit into private practice for the skills and experience gained from working in a business.

Q4: Nigel, do you have any tips for someone who qualified into contentious work but wants to make the move into non-contentious work, for example, personal injury and commercial?

Nigel: This goes back to what Linda was saying and what I touched on. It is about cultivating relationships and demonstrating why your skills are transferable, which they obviously are, into a non-contentious role. You have to show colleagues or firms that you can make a commitment and demonstrate why you can make a difference if they take you on. I like working with contentious lawyers because of the different aspects of experience they bring to bear and their particular approach to problem solving. It is a selling point. You just need to convert that and cultivate relationships. If you don't know anyone, take the steps to get to know people.

Appendix B

Case studies

Lesley Williams

I qualified in September 1988 having completed articles in two high street practices. I enjoyed my training and had a varied practice, basically dealing with anything that came through the door. My caseload was mainly matrimonial (injunctions, divorces and ancillary matters), personal injury and mental health tribunals but I also worked on my principal's medical negligence cases, employment and some probate. I avoided conveyancing at all costs as I found it very tedious and not at all stimulating.

However, I knew that I wanted to practise criminal law and there was very little available so I joined the Crown Prosecution Service (CPS) in February 1989, intending to stay for a couple of years to get advocacy experience. In fact I stayed for over 20 years, leaving in August 2010 to pursue new opportunities in legal education.

Having worked as a crown prosecutor for several years, in the mid-1990s, I started delivering training to prosecutors and police officers. I was one of the trainers on the first joint Police/CPS training programme on the (then very new) Criminal Procedure and Investigations Act (CPIA) 1996 disclosure provisions and one of a group of 25 lawyers who trained all CPS staff on the Human Rights Act.

With a taste for training, I undertook some training qualifications and then moved into learning and development full-time. I became training principal in 2001 and re-launched the CPS Legal Trainee Scheme which went on to win the LawCareers.Net award for Best Recruiter & Trainer in the public sector four times between 2004 and 2007. As head of legal development I managed a small team of lawyers and support staff developing and delivering (with others) a programme of training for 3,500+ CPS lawyers and paralegals. I then worked on the project to secure rights for Associate Prosecutors to be regulated by (then) ILEX.

I had a brief spell working on a wider Civil Service human resources project, then decided, in my mid-40s, that it was time for a change so I left with a vague idea that I might follow my passion of developing the lawyers of the future.

Since leaving the CPS I have been involved in legal education at all levels from A level to LLB and LPC. I work freelance for several institutions, lecturing, teaching seminars and small groups and assessing skills for LPC students. I have recently completed a postgraduate certificate in education (PGCE) and I am now undertaking coaching qualifications with a view to working with young professionals starting out in their careers.

My tip for anyone wanting a career in law ... don't be put off; if you have the determination to succeed there is no reason why you should not. Seek opportunities, exploit (in a positive way) contacts, know what you want, research your chosen path ... but don't be surprised if different opportunities present themselves.

Tip for getting into criminal law ... go to court! There is no other area of life where you can sit and watch the professionals in action. Talk to ushers (they are in charge) and get yourself seen.

Emma Macpherson

I am an 11-year PQE family solicitor working as a sole practitioner in Berkshire.

My career path is rather unusual in that I left school when I was 17 with six modest 'O' levels – three 'B's and three 'C's and trained and worked as a secretary until I was 19. I then returned to college and did two 'A' levels in a year and applied to university. I attended Reading University to read Modern History and International Politics but left after one year to get married. I had my first child when I was 22 and had two more by the time I was 25 years old.

At 27 I returned to university to do a part time LLB (Hons) at the University of Westminster. I graduated in 1996 and took a year out as my husband had cancer. In 1998/1999 I took a full-time Legal Practice Course at the Oxford Institute of Legal Practice and in 1999 I got a job as a paralegal. After a few months I was taken on as a trainee and completed my training in February 2002. I left the firm where I trained and worked as a full-time family solicitor for another six years in two different firms before being made redundant in 2008. I took a year out and in 2009 I set up my own practice after being asked to take over a file for a friend of mine. Four years later I am still running the practice from home and enjoy a very balanced life. I work the hours I need to work but I am able to travel and do other things when work is not so busy. A long, and at time tortuous route, to a very happy and rewarding place. Not for the fainthearted maybe but an example that you do not have to follow the familiar pattern that everyone else does to have an interesting career in the law.

During my time as a family solicitor I have been the Oxfordshire representative on the Berkshire, Oxfordshire and Buckinghamshire Law Society committee, Practice and Organisational Development (POD) liaison officer for the Berkshire, Buckinghamshire and Oxfordshire Collaborative Law POD, a volunteer at the citizens advice bureau and co-chair of the charity MATCH (mothers apart from their children). I have also been interviewed on Radio 4 and taught at Ruskin College, Oxford.

Linda Chamberlain

I am a human resources (HR) specialist in Land Registry. I qualified in 1982 and worked for a variety of London law firms after doing my articles at Druces and Attlee, a very property-orientated law firm at that time. I moved to Farrer and Co doing trust, private client and conveyancing/property work. I then moved to Oppenhiemer Nathan and Vandyck doing private client property work and finally moved on to Clifford Chance doing more commercial/agricultural property work as well. I was made redundant in 1993 and that opened up a new world because I was free to take a maternity cover post at the Law Society working for the Property and Commercial Committee where I began the quest to regulate will writers, and worked on a new edition of the Con 29. The committees I supported during that period included a Land Registrar and I made joining that organisation my long-term aim. When the maternity cover ended, I joined Lewis Silkin and was responsible for setting up its bulk remortgaging team using a very early version of Deposit Protection Service (DPS). Three years later, I did join Land Registry as part of its central legal team setting the practice for processing casework and developing secondary legislation.

My career at Land Registry has been fantastically varied. I studied for an MBA to enable me to be more confident in in-house advisory work, learning more about each department. I was then seconded to the bill team at the Lord Chancellor's Department to put the land registration bill through Parliament, returning to Land Registry to run the training for both staff and customers about the changes that the bill introduced. I then became involved in improving efficiency in our casework operations. In 2010 in the restructure following the property market crash, I took responsibility for all learning and development and capability strategies as well and started on a two-year Chartered Institute of Personnel and Development (CIPD) HR Diploma, for which I am about to start the last module. I have also begun a level 5 Institute of Leadership and Management (ILM) qualification in coaching which is very rewarding. This week as the HR Director retires, I am taking over as the Grade 6 HR delivery manager covering recruitment, counselling and support services, managerial advice, HR support desk and Employment Tribunal Services along with responsibility for the rollout of lean methodology across HR and for the strategy for HR IT services as we move towards a shared service centre. My strategic focus on our corporate leaders development and skills matrix/standards will change to that of talent management and resourcing strategies. This to me seems at 55 years, the piece that joins all my skills together. The legal training has always stood me in good stead, seeing both sides and acting with integrity and impartiality throughout.

My tip – when someone who knows you offers you the chance to do something new, trust his or her judgment and go for it as it is difficult to persuade those who don't know you to give you the same chance.

Sarah Staines

I am a solicitor running my own niche commercial, intellectual property and IT law practice. I left school aged 18 in 1975. After five years in commerce (in business administration and office management) I started in the law in 1980, working for the Warrants Office at the local police station, preparing cases for magistrates court prosecution, the precursor of the CPS. In 1982, I moved jobs to work as a junior secretary then later as paralegal in a high street practice. My work was mainly in criminal and family law. With encouragement from the senior partner I passed my Institute of Legal Executive exams in 1990 and then the Diploma in Legal Practice in 1995 qualifying as a solicitor in 1997. During this study period I worked full-time in commercial litigation, becoming head of department in a large regional firm, during which time I gained a big interest in IT disputes. I took further diplomas in IP law and Business Law and by 1999 had became a partner in that firm and my practice was in the areas of IT/IP/Data Protection. In 2000, I gained a commendation in my Masters Degree in e-commerce law. In 2005, I became a partner in a West London firm. In 2009, I decided to set up my own practice Touchstone Legal Services and now work from home specialising in Commercial, IT and IP law. I have a thriving business and engage three independent consultant solicitors who take on the work they want, work the hours they want, when they want. Although I work far more hours than seems reasonable, I love what I do and the freedom that working for myself brings.

When I started in the law I had no idea that it would lead me to this point. I was not someone who always thought they would be a solicitor. When I was younger I wanted to be an investigative journalist (I think solicitors share much with them, very nosy and with an instinct that things are wrong). Although things have moved on rapidly in the profession since I started out in the law I believe that hard work/preparation and recognising and taking opportunities when they present themselves still has a place in career development. I am happy to share my experience with junior lawyers.

Nigel Hudson

Back in the day they called it 'articles' and I completed mine as an articled clerk with a five-partner firm of solicitors, Ironsides (still a great name), in Leicester.

I had graduated from the University of Leicester, successfully completed my Law Society Finals at the Chester branch of the College of Law, and wanted to return to the city which is still very dear to me. It was 1986, a time of recession not unlike present times, where it was hard work securing what is now known as a training contract. Fortunately, Ironsides took a chance on me and I spent two very happy years there leading up to qualification as a solicitor.

Much to the disappointment of the firm however, I decided to try to get more commercial experience and therefore joined what was then Hepworth & Chadwick (later part of Eversheds) in Leeds as an assistant solicitor in the commercial property department. I hated it. Personality clashes with my principal and an unsupportive environment soon led me back to Leicester and a niche commercial property/planning practice known as Staunton Townshend, which very soon became part of Edge & Ellison (later Hammonds).

I learned a lot at Edge & Ellison but I decided that the route to partnership was not for me. Encouraged by a friend of mine, who had trod a similar path and who was now back at the College of Law only this time as a lecturer, I started to think about branching into professional legal education. Eventually, I managed to obtain a position as a lecturer at Nottingham Law School (NLS), principally teaching property on the newly formed LPC but also contributing to the LLB and GDL teams. Over the course of the next 10 years I moved through the gears from lecturer to senior lecturer to head of the property team, designing and re-designing what became a market leading course and playing a central role in the creation of a new form of LPC specifically for the top city firms. After 10 years however, I felt I'd gone as far as I could at NLS and it was time to move to pastures new, the College of Law.

I've now been working at the College/University of Law for 10 years, 10 years that has seen much change in legal practice, legal education, and the organisation in which I continue to work. At first I was employed as a course designer, later became a practice head, and now I'm the head of learning design with overall responsibility for the organisation's learning and design methodology. It's been an eventful path that's led me to where I am now and a path that I would not have been able to foresee back when I was a mere articled clerk. Who knows what the future holds and that is my advice to any young lawyers: stay focused but keep your vision open, for where you are may not be where you will be.

Appendix C

Useful sources for further information

Organisations

Law Society of England and Wales

www.lawsociety.org.uk
020 7242 1222

Chartered Institute of Legal Executives

www.cilex.org.uk
01234 841000

Solicitors Regulation Authority

www.sra.org.uk
0870 606 2555

The Bar Council

www.barcouncil.org.uk
020 7242 0082

Magistrates' Association

www.magistrates-association.org.uk
020 7387 2353

Crown Prosecution Service

www.cps.gov.uk
020 3357 0000

Government

Government Legal Service

www.gls.gov.uk

Employment

Law Society Gazette Jobs

http://jobs.lawgazette.co.uk

Judicial Appointments Commission (JAC)

http://jac.judiciary.gov.uk

Membership networks

Junior Lawyers Division (JLD)

www.juniorlawyers.lawsociety.org.uk
juniorlawyers@lawsociety.org.uk

Ethnic Minority Lawyers Division

www.lawsociety.org.uk/ethnicminority

Small Firms Division

www.lawsociety.org.uk/smallfirms

In-house Division

www.lawsociety.org.uk/inhouse

Lawyers with Disabilities Division

www.lawsociety.org.uk/lawyerswithdisabilities

Women Lawyers Division

www.lawsociety.org.uk/womensolicitors

Solicitor Judges

www.lawsociety.org.uk/solicitorjudges

Law Society Sections

www.lawsociety.org.uk/communities

Law Society Accreditation Schemes

www.lawsociety.org.uk/accreditation

Junior Chamber International (JCI)

www.jciuk.org.uk
head-office@jciuk.org.uk

Personal development

National Careers Service

https://nationalcareersservice.direct.gov.uk

Higher Apprenticeship in Legal Services

www.legalhigherapprenticeships.com

Chartered Institute of Personal Development

www.cipd.co.uk

Mind Tools

www.mindtools.com

Learn Direct

www.learndirect.co.uk

The Law Society's Diploma in Local Government Law and Practice

www.lawsociety.org.uk/careers/law-graduate-diploma

Law Society CPD Centre

http://cpdcentre.lawsociety.org.uk

Helplines

Law Society Pastoral Care helpline

Help with personal, financial and employment problems
020 7320 5795

Law Society Practice Advice Service

Advice on legal practice and money laundering issues
0870 606 2522

Lawyerline

Advice on client care and complaints handling
0870 606 2588

Professional ethics helpline

Advice on the SRA handbook
0870 606 2577

LawCare

An independent charity part funded by the Law Society offering free and confidential advisory and support service to help lawyers, their staff and their immediate families to deal with health problems such as depression and addiction and related emotional difficulties

0800 279 6888

Solicitors Benevolent Association

Charity providing financial assistance in times of hardship for solicitors and their dependants

020 8675 6440
www.sba.org.uk

Publications

Law Society Gazette

www.lawgazette.co.uk

Chambers Student Guide

www.chambersstudent.co.uk

Training Contract and Pupillage Handbook

www.tcph.co.uk

Law Careers Net

www.lawcareers.net

Law Society Bookshop

http://bookshop.lawsociety.org.uk

Index